Phenomenal Feminine Entrepreneurs

Life-Changing Insights into Taking Control of Your
Prosperity, Your Freedom, & Your Beautiful Future.

CURATED *by* EDWINA MURPHY-DROOMER

Edwina

www.phenomenalfeminineentrepreneurs.com

For every woman who knows
she is meant for more.

Contents

"The truth is, your beliefs are either a ball and chain around your ankles or the seeds that bloom into a beautiful life!"

EDWINA MURPHY-DROOMER

Has hearing somebody else's story ever impacted you to such an extent that it changed your life?

I had just such a moment in October 2018.

Having flown from Australia to America to attend a conference put on by my coach, I was sitting in an audience of about 800 enraptured entrepreneurs as we listened to the stories of six women who had achieved phenomenal success in their business that year.

In my mind, I was thinking, sheesh, imagine that!

The seeds of possibility were being planted...

A few weeks later, I was creating a new vision board for the year ahead and decided to print out a picture of my coach with her arms open in a welcoming gesture whilst standing on stage at THAT conference!

The seeds of possibility were now firmly planted.

It was that vision, my coach's voice, and the tribe around me that pulled me forward through many challenging moments in my newly founded entrepreneurial career, including the death of my beloved sister Phillipa.

Twelve months after those initial seeds had sent their fragile roots into my heart and mind, I walked out onto that stage, in front of a thousand fellow entrepreneurs... filled to overflowing with pride.

I now know with certainty that - who we believe ourselves to be, what we think we're capable of, and the audacity with which we go after our vision - unquestionably determines our prosperity, freedom, and beautiful future.

What I learned is, your beliefs are either a ball and chain around your ankles or the seeds that bloom into a beautiful life!

I created this book, Phenomenal Feminine Entrepreneurs, from a vision I have to plant the seeds of possibility into the hearts and minds of women across the globe.

While listening to Oprah one day, I heard her recite Maya Angelou's poem, Phenomenal Woman. That is how the title for this book came to be.

It is my wish/hope/prayer that by connecting you with the women in this book, women that I so admire, you, too, will feel inspired to reach for bigger, bolder, and more beautiful dreams.

The good news is that the life you dream of living starts with the willingness to unapologetically slide into the driver's seat of your life, to lovingly hold the steering wheel with both hands, and with a clear vision for where you are heading, take off into the great unknown.

I know that with the right beliefs and the right tribe, you can create a life that fills you to overflowing with pride.

Oprah tells us that when she first recited the poem, Phenomenal Woman, in 1978, she didn't believe herself to be a phenomenal woman; she spoke it into being.

And that, dear reader, is what I want for you; to know with certainty that you are a Phenomenal Woman.

So, as you dive into these pages, remember, you've got this, AND we've got you. x

Edwina

www.phenomenalfeminineentrepreneurs.com

Forbes Riley

QUEEN OF THE PITCH WORKING TO
UPLEVEL YOUR GAME! 2.5 BILLION IN
SALES. MOTIVATIONAL KEYNOTE SPEAKER.

Forbes Riley

QUEEN of the PITCH working to UPlevel Your Game!
2.5 Billion in Sales. Motivational Keynote Speaker.

Florida, United States

*"I can clearly say and believe that I am more
than enough and now deserve all the riches
that this glorious life has to offer."*

**What has driven you to create the success that you have?
(What is your WHY?)**

Since I can remember, my mom always wanted to be part of the
glamour of Hollywood, she had autographed photos of the greats,
and it was our pastime to watch the big musicals and dream about
Fred Astaire, Gene Kelly, Cary Grant, Audrey Hepburn and the like.
The Oscars were a highlight for us. As a goofy outcast growing up,
I had stars in my eyes and a burning desire to make my mother happy
- she was an only child of Russian immigrants, and when they both
passed (I was age 4 and my baby sister had just been born), there
was a lingering sadness about her.

My early drivers were to make my mom smile and my dad, the
magician/inventor, proud. I have always been an overachiever with
a fiercely competitive nature. By age 18, I got an invite to the Oscars,
had been in a national beauty pageant on NBS with Bob Hope and
appeared on the $20,000 Pyramid Game Show. Shortly after that, I
worked on Broadway opposite Christopher Reeve, starred in my first
feature film (the classic slasher, Splatter University, and acted in my
mom's favorite soap opera, As The World Turns).

I truly would have loved Julia Roberts or Sandra Bullock's career, but
the universe seemed to have different plans. And I'm grateful they
did. My intensive acting and improv skills combined with a passion for
storytelling have led me on a path of motivational speaker, role model
and CEO of a business training institute that is having more impact on
people's lives than any movie or TV show I could have starred in... and
who knows... it's never too late, as Dame Judi Dench and Helen Mirran
have shown... I may get my Oscar yet!

If you were to choose 3 words that describe who you are as a woman, what would they be?

Passionate, Powerful, Purposeful

What role has vision boards and/or clearly defined goals played in your life and business?

A vision board is a worldly document that transcends time and space. I have been building them since before I can remember and manifesting dreams into reality my entire life. It's beyond magical, and they've been so profound in my life that I created the phrase, Forbesing It - to represent the ability to manifest, especially when NO ONE else thinks it's possible.

I often ask, What Have YOU Forbes'd Lately? Or say I Forbes'd it. I am an artist by nature with a grounded sense of math and numbers. A unique combination as an entrepreneur because while a business may start out as an idea, it remains a hobby or a wish without quantifiable and measurable results.

How do you quieten the shame gremlins that say 'who do you think you are' or 'you're not enough'?

I credit personal breakthrough training with all the genius for lessening the noise in my head. I had imagined an angelic gremlin and a devilish gremlin on either shoulder so many times.

I went through my first immersive transformation when I was 31, and 3 decades later, I have been teaching, coaching, and guiding traumatic childhood breakthrough traumas, and I feel so free, so clear, and ready for action.

I can clearly say and believe that I am more than enough and now deserve all the riches that this glorious life has to offer.

What does living a rich and prosperous life look like to you?

This question is funny as I am answering this question from a self-sustaining ranch high in the Costa Rican mountains. I have been here for a month with my family. We are learning about farming, sourcing natural herbs, food and medicine. Rich is a state of mind, but having passive income fueling my dreams is definitely important. As of late, I finally figured out the online income space, and I'm grateful to my 18-year-old for putting systems and processes in place that allow me to inspire and motivate millions.

Through your feminine lens, what does it mean to be a leader?

As the headliner on stages surrounded by men like Tony Robbins, Grant Cardone, Tai Lopez, Les Brown, Jack Canfield, and Deepak Chopra, being a leader means handling my own and doing it in a tight skirt and high heels. I've devoted a great deal of energy to understanding the masculine and feminine energies in all of us. To be a leader, you don't need to be the strongest or loudest, but you must have clarity, confidence and communication skills.

Male leaders often appear decisive and powerful, and by contrast, a woman may appear weak—quite the contrary. I think being a female leader is a huge advantage; we are by nature intuitive, community-driven and nurturing. This leadership style invokes teamwork and inclusion, resulting in a more inspired and motivated organization.

My personal style is to motivate through transformation and aligning people with their purpose and meaning. Empowering people's attitudes and beliefs, which leads to improved performance. If men spent more time trying to win people's hearts and souls than domination and bravado, they too would be better leaders.

What role has vulnerability played in your success story?

Vulnerability has been a lifelong journey for me. When I was little, I was always told I had a wall around me, and no one could see the real me - no wonder, I was embarrassed, ashamed and confused about the ME they all wanted to see. But, decades of self-discovery, breakthroughs and soul-searching awakenings have led me back to that word vulnerability.

It turns out vulnerability is not a sign of weakness and, ironically, maybe my greatest strength. Having the courage after a massive tragedy, frustration and failures to show up and be seen when I have no control over the outcome and willing to accept however it lands. Finally embracing the notion that it's okay to ask for help, receive compliments and give more than I get, with no connection to the outcome.

It took raising heart centred boy/girl twins and having a devoted man who loves me unconditionally to understand that when I really opened my heart - it didn't shatter... but began to heal and inspired me to show up and really be seen and heard. It's truly the best part of my life!

What is the most difficult decision you have had to make to pursue your dreams?

One of the most difficult decisions was walking away from my acting career and moving my family from Los Angeles to St Petersburg, Florida. I had the lead in a TV series for Fox, about to shoot 65 one-hour episodes and culminate a 2-decade acting career. Then, in a last-minute decision, the executives decided I wasn't famous enough, and they needed a "star" to headline and replaced me with Bo Derek. It shattered my heart and my faith in Hollywood. My agent sealed the departure by saying, "Kiddo, you should brand yourself, you're great... but at 40, if you're no box office gold, they won't want you.

You make all this money from infomercials and home shopping, brand yourself, make your fortune and buy your own movie if you still want it.

Talk about a premonition and a manifestation directive. Today I own a fitness empire and am the CEO of the Billionaire Business Academy. Do I miss acting? Yes. So I do it -- this year, I shot a co-star role in Hallmark's "A Taste of Romance" and the limited series, Transcend. It was the right decision at the time, and I don't look back; the view is much brighter ahead of me!

What are your core guiding values, and why?

Authenticity, Compassion, Consistency, Adventurousness, Spontaneity, and Not Taking ANY of this too seriously.

In my personal life, my values are family, love, health, integrity and fierce loyalty.

What makes you come alive?

Knowing I'm making an impact and a difference. I can chat on Clubhouse and drop nuggets or answer questions for 12 hours straight (and I have), watching the magical transformation of one of my students during my live breakthroughs, getting a hug by my son and daughter and crawling into my man's massive arms and feeling his heartbeat and tender lips.

What self-love rituals do you prioritise and why?

I love my saunas, hot tubs and massages. I have several haunts from the Beverly Hot Springs to the volcano mineral springs in La Fortuna, Costa Rica. I strongly believe in being fit and healthy to be happy. I SpinGym EVERY DAY, and since it's portable, I get a great pilates based workout on an airplane, hotel room or the beaches of the world. I don't drink -- that is absolute self-love and to kiss my man... OFTEN!

What is your favourite strategy to unhook from procrastination?

My daughter has created a strategy I implement called G.S.D. (Get Sh*t Done!) on a project management system and being organized really helps. I love what I do, love my life, and learned that Finishing is Happiness and Not to Let the Perfect Ruin the Good.

> *"... I just love what I do, I love my life and I learned that Finishing is Happiness and Not to Let the Perfect Ruin the Good."*

What would you say to the women who feel they should be able to do-it-all without a tribe/community/coach?

When you're drinking coffee, you don't see the writing outside the cup, but it's easy for others to read it. That's the value of a coach. It was a transformation seminar that completely changed my life along with mentors, accountability partners and masterminds -- you can do it all when you start out small, but to scale and grow, you cannot, nor should you do it alone -- CEO's don't empty the trash cans. Decide what you really want, then learn to work SMARTER, not HARDER.

What are you most grateful for?

I'm grateful for my health, my attitude, my Joshua, my children, all the people I have loved and the ones who have loved me. This life has been a roller coaster, and I wouldn't have missed the ride for anything - the ups, the downs, the turnarounds --, and now I'm grateful that people want to hear me tell stories about it -- it's just SUCH A BLESSING.

What are your guilty pleasures?

Staying in bed with my husband till 11 am and just kissing and cuddling, 2-hour deep tissue massages and mineral springs; I've crossed the globe to soak in the most healing waters from Costa Rica to Corfu, Greece.

What qualities do you see when you say, "She is a PHENOMENAL WOMAN!"?

A strong, evolved, mature woman who has been through hell and back -- who rose from the ashes to pave the way for the next generation of women. A woman who held strong in the wake of being in a man's world, for being bullied about being overweight, who challenged the status quo and when the road ended... paved a new one made of golden bricks that glow in the dark!

Forbes Riley Links

instagram.com/forbes_riley

youtube.com/forbesriley

www.forbesriley.com

facebook.com/forbesriley

twitter.com/forbesriley

@forbersriley

www.forbesriley.TV

A strong, evolved, mature woman who has been through hell and back – who rose from the ashes to glory pave a way for the next generation of women. A woman who held strong in the wake of being in a man's world, for being bullied about being overweight, who challenged the status quo and when the road ended... paved a new one made of golden bricks that glow in the dark!

FORBES RILEY

Annie Grace

AUTHOR & FOUNDER OF THIS NAKED MIND.

Annie Grace

Author & Founder of This Naked Mind.

Colorado, United States

*"What we do through conversation is everything.
We sharpen each other. We open new possibilities.
We awaken curiosity. We learn the next right step
or the next book we want to read or the next person
we want to look to."*

**What has driven you to create the success that you have?
(What is your WHY?)**

My why is really my own journey, initially toward freedom from alcohol.
It's continuously propelled by seeing others find freedom. Specifically,
the few times that I have gotten a letter or a phone call from a child
who is thanking me because they have their mother back. There was
a mother and daughter who came to one of our live events and I
subsequently had them on the This Naked Mind podcast - for a child
to have their parent back and the gift that is for both of them, that
really motivates me. That, and the knowledge that if we can change
this for one generation, we can change it forever.

**If you were to choose 3 words that describe who you are as a
woman, what would they be?**

Willing, driven, and curious.

**What role has vision boards and/or clearly defined goals played
in your life and business?**

I have actually never used a vision board.

**How do you quieten the shame gremlins that say 'who do you
think you are' or 'you're not enough'?**

I use the ACT Technique. ACT stands for Awareness, Clarity,
Turnaround and is key to examining our thoughts and beliefs about
things. I start by writing down those thoughts.

Then, I come back and look at them through the lens of how they
make me feel and how they make me behave. And, if they're not
serving me, then I look for a belief that is more aligned with the truth
- not necessarily the opposite of what those "gremlins" are telling me,
but just something more inclined to propel vs. stifle me.

What does living a rich and prosperous life look like to you?

A rich and prosperous life looks like being really present. I had the unique experience at 33 years old when I looked around at my life and realized I'd really gotten everything I have been striving for, I had a really successful career. I was married to a man I love. I had two kids. I had a beautiful house in the mountains. I had two dogs. And, I wasn't happy. I wasn't present and I wasn't at peace.

So, I think my self-medication with alcohol was not only kicked off but also exacerbated in that one moment - thinking that if everything I thought would get me where I want to be isn't working, then there is no hope for me. It was a really dark place. And, so, for me my whole definition of what rich and prosperous means has changed.

The actor Jim Carrey said, "I think everybody should get rich and famous and do everything they ever dreamed of so they can see that it's not the answer."

That's the moment when real, internal growth awakens. For me, rich looks like being able to drive my son to school at 7:00 a.m. and be completely in appreciation of the conversation we're having and the scenery outside and the fact that it's warm in the car. It's the moments - and, they always bring me back to centre.

Through your feminine lens, what does it mean to be a leader?

When I think about leadership, I go to the idea of living in the radical middle between the tension of self and the tension of togetherness. As women we tend to move more into the togetherness realm, we tend to move more into pleasing and accommodating everyone and everything else. Or, we boomerang and go completely into the self realm where we rely only on ourselves. And, I have done both things.

So now, for me, learning to be in that radical middle of being both deeply connected to other people and deeply connected to myself, living in a way that's driven by my principles instead of my emotions is the most important thing. I might feel really strong emotions - like I don't want to do the next thing or something terrifies me or something is boring - but I have done a lot of work to put in place principles that override those emotions.

One of those is to feel the fear and, if it's right, do it anyway. Because I have decided to live life according to that principle instead of according to that emotion or fear, I often experience a vulnerability hangover and I may overextend myself. It can be really intense, but I know that I did what was right according to my principles. At the same time, I honor my emotions - they are the guide to any work I need to do on my thinking. I don't ignore or suppress my emotions, but I use them as tools. So, I don't know if it's through a feminine lens or not, but that's what leadership looks like to me.

What role has vulnerability played in your success story?

I think all of my success is driven by vulnerability. I remember the first time I got a message from someone on LinkedIn that said something like, "I care about you so I just want to let you know that with what you posted recently you are basically committing career suicide," when I shared my struggles with drinking. I hadn't seen it that way. I just felt like I was doing the next right thing. And, when I looked at it through that lens, I saw she was right. I used to get calls from recruiters for high-level jobs every week ... and they all just dried up when I started to talk about my journey with alcohol. Ultimately, vulnerability really became a superpower.

Whether being interviewed or interviewing others, what role have these connected conversations played in your business?

What we do through conversation is everything. We sharpen each other. We open new possibilities. We awaken curiosity. We learn the next right step or the next book we want to read or the next person we want to look to. It becomes the huge web, this huge network where we can pull on or follow new threads to go in different directions. Those conversations are vital to everything and have been a huge part of my growth.

What is the most difficult decision you have had to make to pursue your dreams?

I think it was making the decision to go against what was safe - what was safe in terms of career and how exposed and vulnerable I was going to be about what was going on inside me and what was safe financially - all of those decisions were needed to move forward into what I thought was the right thing to do. Although I have to say, this was never my dream.

I never envisioned creating what I have in the world. If you had ever told me I would be the one doing this work, I would have laughed you out of the room.

But, I have always been willing. And, I am willing to do the thing that I think I am supposed to do next - the thing that is in my heart. At 33 I realized all the things I thought were my dream had come true - and that's what set me up to be willing.

What are your core guiding values and why?

- Be a peaceful, non-anxious presence
- Prioritize joy and playfulness
- Trust
- Do not be afraid
- Relationships first
- Seek wisdom

What makes you come alive?

The thing that makes me come alive almost more than anything else is discovering connections. And, my favorite kinds of connections to discover are between science and ancient wisdom and grace. When I see one of those connections and have that aha moment, I then create content out of it. It's just really amazing - it brings me alive. That level of curiosity and learning and having to ask all the questions before finding all the answers, researching and then being able to make those connections - I just love that. Relationships also bring me to life - having fun, being present with people.

What self-love rituals do you prioritise and why?

My top two are exercise and meditation/prayer. I meditate/pray once, often twice, a day and I exercise pretty much every single day. It's usually weight lifting, high-intensity interval training, Peloton, Taekwondo. But it can also be stretching, yoga, going for a walk. It is how I manage anxiety, so it is the best way I can take care of myself.

What is your favourite strategy to unhook from procrastination?

Good music and temptation bundles. Temptation bundles are things where we say, "I am going to do these things in order to get this done." Often it's a really yummy snack, maybe some dark chocolate, and some sort of sparkling water or maybe kombucha.

And, I have a very specific playlist I put on when I have to do some hard work. I get both time and space cleared so I can start where I need to start. I allow myself to do the work even if I think it will suck. Usually, the thing that keeps me from doing the work is the belief that I am going to do it wrong, that I am not in the right mindset, that I am going to screw it up. But I know that doing something is always better than doing nothing, even when I am not sure it will be my best.

What would you say to the women who feel they should be able to do-it-all without a tribe/community/coach?

I would invite them to really question that thought. How does it make you feel?

Overwhelmed and stressed, most likely. Frantic. In a hurry. How does it make you behave? Probably not very lovingly. I don't think that hurry and love coexist very well at all. If you know how it makes you feel and behave, you can see the pain of that thought or belief.

And, when you can see the pain of it your brain can very naturally let it go. I would encourage them to try on another thought or belief. That could be, "What I do today will be the most important thing I can get done and if that's lying on the couch watching cartoons with my kid then that's enough."

That's a belief I try on a lot when I feel overwhelmed. Sometimes you have to slow down before you speed up. Sometimes you have to let the balls drop so you can stop juggling and intentionally pick back up only the most important balls. I heard a great analogy once about someone who was running so fast they didn't feel like they could stop and someone came up alongside them and offered them a bicycle.

But the person didn't know how to ride a bicycle and didn't want to stop long enough to learn even though it would help them go faster. The lesson being when you are frantic and in a hurry, learn to pause for a moment and look for a better way to get where you are going. Let that overwhelm be an indicator that you should do the exact opposite of what you think you should do.

Stop and allow yourself to learn how to manage better - how to get leverage, how to find more peace, how to create more energy, how to create drive. I think that's the secret - that we don't need to always be doing more, pushing more against something that's going to break; it's finding a different way.

For me, that has always been with a lot of space and a lot of margin and a lot of time. People would be really surprised if they saw a day in my life. There is a lot of space-time for meditation, journaling, hanging out with my kids, exercise. And I probably get more done than most people I know but I have always stopped to learn how to ride the bicycle - learning how to leverage a team and finding different ways to do more with what I have. There is always a bicycle - you just need to take a moment to learn how to ride it.

Whose voices do you tune into for a guaranteed dose of inspiration.

Byron Katie, Eckhart Tolle, my pastor Jay Pathak, Rob Bell

What role have coaches and/or masterminds played in your success?

Coaches and masterminds are key. I make sure to value them, prioritize and meet with them. Masterminds are magical. I am always surprised - even when I don't think I will bring something back, I always do. I have multiple coaches - personal, spiritual, and business. Every two weeks I meet with a different coach for an hour.

Do you think you would be where you are now without having worked with a coach and why or why not?

No way. Coaches have been incredible and I think that is our whole purpose - to learn something and then show others so that our evolution can take an exponential turn because more of us are simplifying things and making it easier and giving. This is vital.

What are you most grateful for?

I am most grateful for grace, for the fact that we are loved unconditionally and that we have been created and for my family.

What are your guilty pleasures?

I really like my kids' television shows like Hannah Montana and Big Time Rush and some of these teeny-bopper shows - so entertaining, no drama, no intensity, no negativity, just super fun. Also, cookie dough is a major guilty pleasure.

What qualities do you see when you say, "She is a PHENOMENAL WOMAN!"?

Phenomenal Woman reminds me of the Maya Angelou poem with the same title. For me, a phenomenal woman is someone who is inspiring and magnetic and makes you feel when you are with them as if you are also inspiring and magnetic; someone who holds others in high regard, not higher than herself because she realizes that she is worthy and that worthiness is inherent; someone who is super courageous, willing to feel the fear and do it anyway; someone who does the right thing even when there is a cost; someone who is motivated by joy and playfulness vs. burning herself out.

Annie Grace Links

instagram.com/thisnakedmind

youtube.com/thisnakedmind

www.thisnakedmind.com

facebook.com/anniegraceauthor

twitter.com/thisnakedmind

Kirsty Wirth

EDUCATOR, INTEGRATIVE HEALTH COACH
& THE FOUNDER OF KULTURED WELLNESS.

Kirsty Wirth

Educator, Integrative Health Coach
& the founder of Kultured Wellness.

Queensland, Australia

"It feels like my whole business has thrived through connection. I don't network; I connect, and the connections that have played the biggest part in driving the success of my business..."

What has driven you to create the success that you have? (What is your WHY?)
My son was originally my why and now it's just the whole world!!!!! And from what he and my family have been through and the gains we have made it really is my mission and purpose to ensure that the world knows that there is another way, that labels and health diagnosis and chronic illness is not something that we should stand for and just accept. It's not normal, and doesn't need to be that way. There is so much that can be done and I want to support everyone to learn the tools, gain the knowledge and implement so that they can find optimal health and achieve their dreams, not just health dreams but life long dreams.

If you were to choose 3 words that describe who you are as a woman, what would they be?
Inspiring, empowering and tenacious.

What role has vision boards and/or clearly defined goals played in your life and business?
A huge role. I don't use vision boards as my kids end up sticking up presents they want!! Hahaha but I am a big fan of goals and project goals and setting targets. A goal is just a dream with a deadline. I have so many dreams and aspirations. What makes them a reality is having the right people around me to work on them, define them, tease them apart into actionable steps, and then measure, measure, measure!! I am a big thinker and visionary person who loves to ponder and think, and I find it really hard to work on small detailed things. Still, they count, so I have people around me who are the direct opposite who love working on the detail, ticking off the action steps and who hold me accountable to get things done.

How do you quieten the shame gremlins that say 'who do you think you are' or 'you're not enough'?

Hmmm, this is a great question. I don't think it will ever be completely quiet, but I have learnt to tame the beast.

1. I make sure I celebrate the wins so I know that I am achieving my mission and goals and doing as much as I can at that point in time.

2. I reflect on our clients' wins and how we have supported them to reach their goals.

3. I focus on my health and exercise to get a brain boost of feel-good chemicals. It works a charm. And of course, I eat fermented foods to create an environment in my gut where I can also make feel-good chemicals such as serotonin and dopamine, so I don't have to rely on willpower or constant affirmations. My body just knows how to make me feel good. The final one is to spend as much time in nature and with family.

What does living a rich and prosperous life look like to you?

Spending time with my family, friends and community, living a simple, sustainable life with minimal waste and consumption, lots of time in nature and free from technology and media, marketing etc. Constantly learning is huge for me, and then spending time unpacking what I have learnt and pondering. Space and time to do this are so important to me. A healthy body that I move regularly and prioritising the food I put into my body and how I nourish myself.

Through your feminine lens, what does it mean to be a leader?

Being curious is my biggest aim as a leader and always assuming I have the most to learn. Empowering others and providing freedom for others to show their best, and finding a solution that results in everyone feeling like their voice was heard, that they were safe sharing their feelings.

What role has vulnerability played in your success story?

Oh gosh, sharing my story and what has happened to myself and my children has been huge for me, and I have had to be so vulnerable and ok with that. I know that it enables people to connect. It resonates with so many and supports them to feel the courage that they need to make changes and to step away from old patterns and belief systems. Still, wow, I find it confronting sharing my heart and soul, but I work on being vulnerable and doing that as it links back to achieving my purpose and mission, so I work on it every day.

Whether being interviewed or interviewing others, what role have these connected conversations played in your business?

It feels like my whole business has thrived through connection. I don't network; I connect, and the connections that have played the biggest part in driving the success of my business have been from spending quality time together, often in nature, free from outside noise, and it leads to so much success. I don't often respond to social media reach outs or people who want me to share products, etc., as if there is no integrity or common goal that is bigger than making sales or profit; I am just not interested.

What is the most difficult decision you have had to make to pursue your dreams?

Funnily enough, I don't see any decisions that I have made being difficult. If they align and I see the purpose, I generally just get excited about the next adventure that awaits.

There may be hard moments in those decisions, but it's how we frame the outcome and what is needed to get there.

What are your core guiding values, and why?
- Community, family and friends
- Integrity
- Connection
- Being curious
- Questioning the norm and social expectations

What makes you come alive?

Being in nature, my outdoor sports, finding out what my body is capable of. Watching my children grow, learn and shine and watching my clients win and achieve their health goals and seeing gut health gaining momentum and the broader community seeing that our chronic state of health and mental health is from a complete disconnection from nature and real food.

What self-love rituals do you prioritise and why?

Eating real and nourishing foods, including fermented foods, cooking for myself and my family. As much time connecting in with nature as possible. Switching off at night and making sure I get quality sleep. Did I mention I love my sauna!!! Haha. Focusing on quiet time, time to reflect and be curious, and also making sure I breathe and be mindful and have time out.

What is your favourite strategy to unhook from procrastination?

Do a handstand!! No joke, it works every time!!

What would you say to the women who feel they should be able to do-it-all without a tribe/community/coach?

Well, apart from the fact it's impossible it's also just really boring!! Hahaha. How do you share your wins? Where do the laughs, tears, and fun come from if you are slogging at it on your own? And I always make the assumption I know nothing and have so much to learn and can't wait to meet someone who can share their knowledge and teach me.

Whose voices do you tune into for a guaranteed dose of inspiration?

I still listen to my Papa's inspirational teachings. He has passed away now, but he is always with me and such an inspiration. My clients also often write about their wins and achieve their goals, and gosh, it just motivates me to continue.

What role have coaches and/or masterminds played in your success?

A huge role. As I mentioned above, I literally couldn't have achieved anything through my business had it not been for coaches and mentors. When I know I have a goal I want to achieve and work out what steps I need to take to get to it, I then reach out to the expert in that field and ask so many questions and milk them dry of their knowledge (haha) so I can reach my goal. There are so many people out there with so much knowledge and expertise that it's exciting to meet them and learn for them.

Do you think you would be where you are now without having worked with a coach and why or why not?

I don't think so. I started Kultured Wellness with no idea about the online world, how to run a business, how to work a budget etc. I literally had no idea, so in every aspect of my business, I have reached out to the best and learned from them, and it's been so amazing.

What are you most grateful for?

My son's recovery, my health recovery and my journey. That I am alive after living through the boxing day Tsunami and that my husband and I broke the pattern and became curious about how to help our family, and that we keep going and are now reaping the rewards.

What are your guilty pleasures?

All the same as my self-love rituals!!!! They all feel so good to me; they are like a guilty pleasure.

What qualities do you see when you say, "She is a PHENOMENAL WOMAN!"?

Courageous, curious, vulnerable, comfortable learning and not know everything, comfortable taking what is needed for herself and growth but also very focused on giving back to the community. Someone full of love and curiosity about the world and lacking in judgement and that there is a right and wrong way to approach the world.

Kirsty Wirth Links

📷 *instagram.com/kulturedwellness*

📘 *facebook.com/kulturedwellness*

🌐 *www.kulturedwellness.com*

Courageous, curious, vulnerable, comfortable learning and not know everything, comfortable taking what is needed for herself and growth but also very focused on giving back to the community. Someone full of love and curiosity about the world and lacking in judgement and that there is a right and wrong way to approach the world.

KIRSTY WIRTH

Dr. Marcy Cole Ph.D.

HOLISTIC PSYCHOTHERAPIST, SPEAKER,
AUTHOR, COMMUNITY MOBILIZER,
HUMANITARIAN, VISIONARY AND
WELLNESS EDUCATOR.

Dr Marcy Cole Ph.D.

Holistic Psychotherapist, Speaker, Author,
Community Mobilizer, Humanitarian,
Visionary and Wellness Educator.

California, United States

*"Our vulnerability reflects our capacity to
access the deepest recesses of our mind and
withstand our hearts breaking open."*

**What has driven you to create the success that you have?
(What is your WHY?)**
I remember as a child thinking about wanting to "make a contribution".
I didn't know what it meant then, but this has been the consistent
motivator... to be of service in my work ... that makes sense to my
conscience, and feels good in my heart.

**If you were to choose 3 words that describe who you are as a
woman, what would they be?**
Insightful, Heart-centred, Powerful

**What role has vision boards and/or clearly defined goals played
in your life and business?**
I share with my clients that you need to believe to receive.
Envisioning is the first step to getting there.

**How do you quieten the shame gremlins that say 'who do you
think you are' or 'you're not enough'?**
Because the human experience is mostly a collective experience,
I remind myself there is little original self-development content that
has not yet already been shared, in one form or another. I also remind
myself that what comes through every individual is still originally
unique. *Who receives our messages, creations and innovations, and
when they do, is a function of time, sacred synchronicity and destiny.
Thus, who are we not to share whatever may have a legacy impact
on another sweet soul in the world.*

What does living a rich and prosperous life look like to you?

Abundance + Gratitude in every area of life: Health, Love, Community Career, Financial

Through your feminine lens, what does it mean to be a leader?

It takes Vision, Direct & Respectful Expression, + Steadfast and Flexible Action.

Setting boundaries without Bullying, Motivating others through Inspiring versus intimidating, Encouraging Verses Pressuring, Coaching/Teaching versus Imposing, Helping amplify faith versus fear in all we touch.

What role has vulnerability played in your success story?

I love Gandhi's saying, "My Life is My Message". Our vulnerability reflects our capacity to access the deepest recesses of our mind and withstand our hearts breaking open. It is the portal to the truth that is revealed through this deeper dive and opening. We get there when we soar in our most brilliant light and when we are brought to our knees through heartbreak and humility.

I have tried to access the lessons learned from "mis-takes" and wisdom from my wounds and bring them into my guidance work with others. It's such a powerful exchange. For "giving liberates the soul of the giver", as Maya Angelou said...while - as others learn to receive, they feel less alone, with greater agency to access and express the portals of their own heart. And then, the giving wisdom circle continues...

Whether being interviewed or interviewing others, what role have these connected conversations played in your business?

We are all on this journey as humans together. Whether it's inquiring or sharing...

it's a feedback loop that makes meaning of our individual and collective experiences, which carry the power to heal, connect, remind and inspire one another.

What is the most difficult decision you have had to make to pursue your dreams?

Taking leaps out of the tried, true, lucrative and familiar.. into unknown territory. I've done this a few times...felt some jitters as I leapt and never looked back.

What are your core guiding values, and why?

Truth: Because it's what's real, sets us free, and successfully supports finding opportunities and individuals who are in authentic and congruent alignment with our core values and vision.

Community: Because it's the most powerful form of currency we have.

Meaningful Work: Because otherwise, it's just work! For me, spending time "working" on anything without it carrying the potential for positive impact... is empty calories for the soul.

Fun: Play and Laughter is part of our DNA, birthright, and life force energy. It lifts our mood, brightens our energy field and brings levity to even the hardest of times.

We need this to enjoy life, transcend challenges, and thrive in spite of them.

Love: Because I believe that loving and being loved is what life is truly all about.

What are the top 3 things that make you come alive?

- LOVING EXCHANGES
- BELLY LAUGHTER
- MEANINGFUL CONTRIBUTION TO HUMANITY

What self-love rituals do you prioritise and why?

I say YES as often as possible to things that intrigue, educate, inspire, pamper and entertain me.

I say NO to that which does not align and to those with whom I do not feel a genuine connection.

What is your favourite strategy to unhook from procrastination?

Good Night Sleep...Early Morning Productivity... Get the stuff done first you don't want to do...because it frees our minds and energy field to get to the stuff that matters most.

What would you say to the women who feel they should be able to do-it-all without a tribe/community/coach?

You can only go so far alone. Coaching helps point out blind spots and teaches what you do not know. Community bears witness...and holds space for support and celebration of who you and your intentions.

Whose voice/s do you tune into for a guaranteed dose of inspiration?

Oprah, Rev. Michael Beckwith, Elizabeth Gilbert

What role have coaches and/or masterminds played in your success?

Not enough! Meaning... I could still use more to reach new heights of awareness, productivity and visibility by working with a coach.

Mastermind groups have been so valuable to be a resource and cheering squad for one another.

Do you think you would be where you are now without having worked with a coach and why or why not?

I've had countless notable transformational teachers on the stages of the Life Enrichment Events I produce. So through osmosis, I have received so much from all of them. Sometimes, it's hard to know where we'd be because our conscious, subconscious, and even unconscious always listen and integrate what we are exposed to. I just know I'm thankful for it all!

What are you most grateful for?

For being cradled in love my whole life.

What are your top 3 guilty pleasures?

I don't feel guilty for any pleasures.

What qualities do you see when you say, "She is a PHENOMENAL WOMAN!"?

Wise, Creative, Courageous, Expressive, Resilient, Impactful, Loving

Dr Marcy Cole Links

📷 *instagram.com/Cole.Marcy*　　　▶ *youtube.com/drmarcycole*

📘 *facebook.com/DrMarcyCole*　　　🌐 *www.DrMarcyCole.com*

Kim Morrison

BREAKTHROUGH COACH AND MENTOR,
NLP MASTER PRACTITIONER AND
HYPNOTHERAPIST, BEST-SELLING
AUTHOR, & FOUNDER OF TWENTY.8.

Kim Morrison

Breakthrough Coach and Mentor, NLP Master
Practitioner and Hypnotherapist, Best-selling
Author, & Founder of Twenty.8.

Queensland, Australia

*"Vulnerability can be my greatest super-power.
When I share my truth with strength and
love, when I can stand on the other side of
fear and share my learnings and stories, I get
to share the real me. "*

**What has driven you to create the success that you have?
(What is your WHY?)**
When I started my business, I wanted to be the largest aromatherapy
company in the southern hemisphere. As time went on, I realised
my true reason, my real why, was to support one woman at a time to
tap into their innate healing power, to nourish and nurture her family
through the medicinal qualities of plants, herbs, essential oils and
nature. Beyond that, my bigger why has always been to create a
beautiful legacy for my family and children.

**If you were to choose 3 words that describe who you are as
a woman, what would they be?**
Resilient, tenacious and caring.

**What role has vision boards and/or clearly defined goals played
in your life and business?**
These are huge to me. I love my SMART goals and vision boards.
I turned to creating online mind movies that I watch at the start
of most days. All of these things keep me on target and focused
on completing things I need to do. I love the big picture thinking
and dreaming, and I love the finer details and ticking off tasks as
completed. Maybe as a former international athlete, I also love
having goals and setting myself targets within time frames so I can
achieve more.

How do you quieten the shame gremlins that say 'who do you think you are' or 'you're not enough'?

I must admit I have done a lot of work on myself over the years, and thankfully they do not appear the way they may have in the past.

I know I feel at my worst when I compare myself to others, so I quickly move away from that if I notice myself feeling down or not good enough.

Being an NLP Master Practitioner and Hypnotherapist, I also have several techniques to clear negative thinking and limiting thoughts and beliefs. I am so grateful for the coaching I receive and that I love to stay in the work of self-improvement.

What does living a rich and prosperous life look like to you?

Being fit, healthy and happy. Making money is one aspect of being rich but having travelled to many third world countries, having seen what happens when people lose their vitality, confidence and health and understanding how no amount of money can pay for these things, quickly reminds me that being rich and prosperous is not what I might have thought it was when I was young.

Through your feminine lens, what does it mean to be a leader?

To go first, to offer myself in all capacity and give it everything I have. To have courage, grace, strength and dignity. To be my best self by standing strong, walking my talk, being vulnerable, taking care and being kind.

What role has vulnerability played in your success story?

Vulnerability can be my greatest super-power. When I share my truth with strength and love, when I can stand on the other side of fear and share my learnings and stories, I get to share the real me. And in doing so, others then share the same. Barriers come down, and we connect in a much deeper and more profound way. I truly believe the more vulnerable, the more connection there is.

Whether being interviewed or interviewing others, what role have these connected conversations played in your business?

They are everything. Connected conversations mean we get directly to the heart, the core of one another. We get to share ourselves more expansively and honestly and without doubt, it is these open-hearted, courageous conversations that allow you to just be yourself in an authentic, loving and respectful way.

What is the most difficult decision you have had to make to pursue your dreams?

Asking to buy a business partner out was extremely difficult and heart-wrenching. I thought we might be able to do it with grace and love, but it was incredibly hurtful and challenging.

Some things I could have done way better, some things I felt so proud of, yet none of it was easy, emotions were high, and there were many people's feelings and lives to consider. I felt terrible making this decision, but I knew deep in my heart it was absolutely necessary for me and for the business to grow.

What are your core guiding values, and why?

I have four guiding business principles that I have stuck to throughout my business, and they are:

Connect

Connection is the life force of a business. Connecting with your precious customers and understanding their desires, needs and problems. Creating healthy relationships with your contractors and manufacturers. Honouring your incredibly special team members and valuing your community are all essential. And most importantly, connection within, connection with your goals, and your 'why' are what will get you up each day.

Care

Take care of your business. Love her up. Appreciate she is the entity in which you get to live your passion. Show you care for what happens within your business from the team and your products, right through to the customer. Most importantly, take care of yourself.

Self-care is not selfish; it's essential. If you do not take care of yourself, you might not have the health and energy to sustain all that your beautiful business needs.

Collaborate

I have learned in business that you are not alone, people are willing to help, and you only have to ask. Working with others for the greater good, joining forces and collaborating in a synergistic way is incredibly empowering. Collaboration is now something I rate as an integral part of the business.

Contribute

Giving back, helping others, enjoying the journey. Ultimately this is what my business is all about. Being able to create a profitable entity means I can help others. Being able to offer scholarships to my programs, products to charities, and my time for worthy causes is one of the most liberating parts of what I do. It's the old adage – the more you give, the more you receive.

What makes you come alive?

Being in nature, running, seeing my family happy and healthy, watching my kids achieve their dreams, being in my home, feeling fit and healthy, travelling, sharing meals and good times with family and friends, adventure, music, working on my business, speaking on stage, seeing my products with happy customers, releasing new products, creating new programs and writing new books, mentoring my clients and hearing from people who have had their lives changed thanks to something I may have contributed towards. There are literally so many things that make me feel alive. I think I have gratitude for all things that feed my soul.

What self-love rituals do you prioritise and why?

Considering my business is all about the importance of self-love and providing the tools of self-care it is important to me that I authentically walk my talk. Self-care rituals are non-negotiable. After all, you cannot give from an empty cup. I love my essential oil daily body boost ritual, which I have been doing every day since 1987. I love daily skincare rituals. I love to put on my diffuser and create the mood and energy for everyone in my home and office. Movement and exercise are a huge priority for my self-love rituals. Reading something every day. Writing in my gratitude journal or messaging my hubby when he is away, the things we are grateful for that day. Food is a massive part of self-love for me. I will always prioritise getting to the farmer's markets each week, buying as natural and organic as possible, supporting our local providers, making beautiful, healthy meals and taking care of my mind, body and skin.

What is your favourite strategy to unhook from procrastination?

I look over my Life Values and my SMART goals as I find that is the quickest way to get focused again. It helps me to connect back to what is important to me and what I want to achieve. And if procrastination persists, I will go for a run and then look at my Values and SMART goals again.

What would you say to the women who feel they should be able to do-it-all without a tribe/community/coach?

Good on them. Some businesses may just require the simplicity of being a solo entrepreneur. I personally love being part of a team; even if it is small, I love being a part of different communities and creating communities for my clients and customers. And I have certainly appreciated having a business coach and mentor throughout most of my entrepreneur life.

Whose voices do you tune into for a guaranteed dose of inspiration?

My inner circle. It could be my besties, coach, mentor, business partner, family, kids, and/or husband. Each offers different insights; each knows I love to be coached and supported, and each of them inspires me to be a better version of myself at all times.

What role have coaches and/or masterminds played in your success?

A huge amount. It is hard to walk in unknown and unchartered territory without the support and advice of those who have. For a while, I did it alone, implementing the learnings from various courses, programs and therapists, and my passion for growing my business.

When I took on a business coach and mentor, my business grew 400% in one year. He pushed me, challenged me and believed in me. It's a bit like having a PT or sports coach.

They can set the challenge, they know how to push you, they can show you a strategy and program and check in with you, driving you further than you might ever imagine alone. It's amazing to have someone you can look up to, question, and pose different scenarios. It's also great to know someone is in your corner and wants you to succeed. Someone who can help enhance emotional intelligence. And someone to monitor risk and avoid what my business coach called 'dumb tax'.

Do you think you would be where you are now without having worked with a coach and why or why not?

My gut says a big no! It certainly may have taken a lot longer without one. I just love the accountability, support, care, knowledge and insights. I personally think it's imperative.

What are you most grateful for?

My amazing husband and children. My health. My family and friends. My business and my clients. I can list so many things, but given these strange times we are all living through, I would have to say living down under (Australia) is also a blessing I do not take for granted.

What are your guilty pleasures?

I'm not sure I have guilty pleasures. I own every one of the pleasures I indulge in. No time for guilt!

What qualities do you see when you say, "She is a PHENOMENAL WOMAN!"?

I think every woman is phenomenal in some way or another. And as I think of all the phenomenal women I know, I just see all their greatness. I see that she is inspirational and leads by example. She is influential. She learns from her mistakes and gets up after every set-down. She knows she has constraints and weaknesses, but she is willing to work on them.

She has lashings of self-respect and self-discipline. She has courage, grace, strength and dignity. She is brave and vulnerable. She is intelligent. She is beautiful inside and out. She cares. She is kind. She accepts herself for who she is. A phenomenal woman is the fullest expression of self-love.

Kim Morrison Links

instagram.com/kimmorrison28   twitter.com/kimmorrison28   www.kimmorrison.com

facebook.com/KimMorrisonTraining   www.twenty8.com

Eva Nedilek

CERTIFIED HIGH-PERFORMANCE COACH.

Eva Medilek

Certified High-Performance Coach.

California, United States

"I was done working to make others wealthy. I was too old to ask permission to live a life I loved. It was time for me to take control of how I want to live."

What has driven you to create the success that you have? (What is your WHY?)

In a word, freedom. The freedom to choose what, where and when to do whatever I want to do. When I was working as a dental hygienist, the humiliation I felt in asking for "time off" to be sick, visit family, travel or even attend the funerals of loved ones felt so constricting. I longed to live and work in a country where you had time off to do these things. And, I know if I wanted that freedom of choice lifestyle, I would have to create it myself. Being downsized at work with my salary cut while my employer was buying new cars and taking fancy vacations was the fire that sparked my journey of entrepreneurship. I was done working to make others wealthy. I was too old to ask permission to live a life I loved. It was time for me to take control of how I want to live.

If you were to choose 3 words that describe who you are as a woman, what would they be?

Open, Connected, Generous.

What role has vision boards and/or clearly defined goals played in your life and business?

I love vision boards and writing down my goals for my business clearly. When I don't do that, I lose focus on my priorities and become easily distracted. When my goals are clear, it's easy to make the necessary decisions to move them forward and not get off track.

How do you quieten the shame gremlins that say 'who do you think you are' or 'you're not enough'?

Reading. I read an average of 2 books per month for personal growth and development.

I'm not the only one with this mind chatter, and I'm constantly listening to other successful women and learning from them what they've done and continue to do to move forward despite the chatter and the feelings of "not enoughness". I also PRACTICE gratitude, and I honor the women in my lineage who sacrificed so that each generation can have it better than they did. I owe it to them to not let the chatter stop me. I recognize that the chatter is there; I notice it and continue forward anyway.

What does living a rich and prosperous life look like to you?

Back to freedom of choice. Specifically around food and health choices. Yes, the nice home and vacation experiences are a part of it. But the real motivation to live rich and prosperous is to have true food and health security. You cannot be your best unless you feel your best.

Through your feminine lens, what does it mean to be a leader?

Courage. The courage to be uncomfortable. The courage to be heard because what you have to say matters. The courage to walk your talk and to be in full transparency and integrity. The courage to create opportunities for others to be seen and heard that do not have fair and equitable opportunities.

What role has vulnerability played in your success story?

A huge part of my success story centres around WHO I was being in my relationship with my husband while building a successful business. I was in a constant state of stress, frustration and overwhelm and the energy around me was not fun.

My husband fell in love with another woman during that time, and I had to face my responsibility in that infidelity.

It wasn't easy to look at myself that deeply and know that I shared responsibility in the breakdown of my marriage. It's also the reason that we have broken through and have a better relationship now.

Whether being interviewed or interviewing others, what role have these connected conversations played in your business?

People can see themselves in the story that I share, and it causes them to take responsibility for who they are being. The foundation of my work is to look at how our early life experiences have formed our habits, patterns, beliefs, and behaviors and what role that plays in damaging our relationships.

What is the most difficult decision you have had to make to pursue your dreams?

I would say it was making a significant financial investment in myself and my business, knowing that my husband wouldn't fully support me spending the money.

What are your core guiding values, and why?

Honesty, integrity and service. How you do one thing is how you do everything. I would never coach anyone to do anything I haven't done or wouldn't do myself. My word is my bond, and I'm loyal and fight for my clients and their success. I couldn't coach if I didn't believe in the power of coaching. I coach, I have coaches, and I am coachable.

What top 3 things make you come alive?

Movement; I love to move my body and generate energy. My dog; she literally lights me up. Client success; when my clients have a breakthrough, I do a happy dance with my dog around the coffee table. It's the best feeling in the world.

What self-love rituals do you prioritise and why?

My morning routine. I set myself up to have the mental energy and physical stamina to win the day.

I trampoline, meditate, practise gratitude, set the day's intention and drink my lemon/apple cider vinegar drink. Taking care of my mind, body and spirit is the highest form of self-love for me. And.... my eyelashes lol.

What is your favourite strategy to unhook from procrastination?

I plan my day in time blocks. I turn off distractions that may cause procrastination, and then I take a break every hour to re-energize and reset. I also have an accountability buddy for the bigger projects.

What would you say to the women who feel they should be able to do-it-all without a tribe/community/coach?

You are setting yourself up to fail and/or feel like a failure. We go further faster with a crew. Look at the high-performance race cars on the racetrack. When they stop for a pitstop, a full crew is working to make sure that the car finishes strong without breaking down on the track. The driver isn't getting out and changing the tires. You are sacrificing what is really important when you try to do it all yourself.

Whose voice/s do you tune into for a guaranteed dose of inspiration?

I love listening to and reading Brene Brown as well as Jen Sincero.

What role have coaches and/or masterminds played in your success?

Everything. I could not have the perspective and skill set to level up my performance without my coaches and mentors.

Do you think you would be where you are now without having worked with a coach and why or why not?

Absolutely not. Coaches collapse time frames. I was already in my 50's before starting my entrepreneurial journey. I did not have the luxury of time. Investing in coaches and mentors allowed me to achieve my success within a 3-5 year period and continues to grow me as a person as well as my business. I will always have a coach.

What are you most grateful for?

I'm grateful that I invested in myself. If I hadn't, this past year of lockdowns would have been devastating to my family and me. My personal development and leadership training has allowed me to thrive in this situation with my business, relationships and health, stronger than ever.

What are your top 3 guilty pleasures?

Ooo, that's a good one: people magazine, any cookie and eyelash extensions.

What qualities do you see when you say, "She is a PHENOMENAL WOMAN!"?

Resilience, leadership, femininity and pure joy.

Eva Medilek Links

 instagram.com/evamedilekexecutivecoach

 facebook.com/evamedileksuccesscoach

 www.evamedilek.com/youtube

 twitter.com/evamedilek

 www.evamedilek.com

Rachel Pedersen

"THE QUEEN OF SOCIAL MEDIA",
FOUNDER & CEO OF AWARD-WINNING
SOCIAL MEDIA MARKETING AGENCY
THE VIRAL TOUCH, FOUNDER & CEO
OF SOCIAL MEDIA UNITED.

Rachel Pedersen

"The Queen of Social Media" - Founder & CEO of award-winning social media marketing agency The Viral Touch, Founder & CEO of Social Media United.

Greater Minneapolis, United States

"To me, being a leader means to stand in confidence and strength. Even when things around you are broken, you can choose the RIGHT decision, even if you're standing alone."

What has driven you to create the success that you have? (What is your WHY?)

My WHY is my past self. My future self. My kids, and every single woman who wants to dream big!!! I want to inspire, break the mold and create massive success despite my upbringing and past!!!

If you were to choose 3 words that describe who you are as a woman, what would they be?

Kind, fun, and persistent!

What role has vision boards and/or clearly defined goals played in your life and business?

They're everything to me! I post the goals I have all around my house - on my mirrors, on boards, on Pinterest, all around me!!!

How do you quieten the shame gremlins that say 'who do you think you are' or 'you're not enough'?

Meditation is how I quiet the shame gremlins, and then I listen to affirmations that remind me EXACTLY who I am!

What does living a rich and prosperous life look like to you?

Living a rich and prosperous life looks like a freedom filled life. A life of intention based decisions and action steps.

Through your feminine lens, what does it mean to be a leader?

To me, being a leader means to stand in confidence and strength. Even when things around you are broken, you can choose the RIGHT decision, even if you're standing alone. You offer a solution that stands out amidst the confusion of the world.

What role has vulnerability played in your success story?

Vulnerability is my #1 MO (modus operandi) - it's how I operate, and it's how I lead. Even when it's scary, I'm vulnerable about the hardest things in my life and my past.

Whether being interviewed or interviewing others, what role have these connected conversations played in your business?

Building relationships is everything - it's usually the BEFORE and AFTER that develops deep and lasting relationships, so I like to find common ground and discover how we're alike! Relationships can cover a lot of cracks in a business and cover everything like a beautiful epoxy - making rough things smoother.

What is the most difficult decision you have had to make to pursue your dreams?

The most difficult decision I've made to pursue my dreams was letting go of people who weren't aligned with my core values as we grew apart. That's okay - even though it's hard.

What are your core guiding values and why?

1. Honesty

2. Loyalty

3. Consistency

4. Human First

5. Fun

What makes you come alive?

1. Adventure

2. Speaking on stage

3. Being creative

What self-love rituals do you prioritise and why?

Meditation, working out, affirmations, visualization, journals, eating well, baths, reading!!!!

What is your favourite strategy to unhook from procrastination?

I set a timer and turn on motivational music or motivational roundups from YouTube. JUST HIT GO!!!!

What would you say to the women who feel they should be able to do-it-all without a tribe/community/coach?

No one is meant to do it all/be it all alone. Find your people - both your community and your mentor - so you can go further on the journey!

Whose voices do you tune into for a guaranteed dose of inspiration.

I love Lisa Nichols, Shonda Rhimes, Cate Blanchett, Arnold, Sylvester Stallone, and my future self!!!

What role have coaches and/or masterminds played in your success?

Coaches and masterminds have kept me going when I felt like giving up!!! They've helped me break through limiting beliefs and programs, helped me discover new ideas/strategies and helped me to become the BEST version of myself.

Do you think you would be where you are now without having worked with a coach and why or why not?

Absolutely not. Coaches have helped me to shortcut decades in a few days and make me the best version of myself.

What are you most grateful for?

God, myself, my family!!!

What are your guilty pleasures?

1. Ice cream

2. Reality TV

3. Adventure/escape rooms

What qualities do you see when you say, "She is a PHENOMENAL WOMAN!"?

She's strong, confident, vulnerable, fun, kind, gracious, generous, and she sees possibility in everything.

Rachel Pedersen Links

[instagram icon] *instagram.com/themrspedersen*

[facebook icon] *facebook.com/the.mrs.pedersen*

[tiktok icon] *tiktok.com/@themrspedersen*

[twitter icon] *twitter.com/TheMrsPedersen*

[web icon] *www.rachelpedersen.com*

Jasmoyne Blakely

MOTIVATIONAL SPEAKER, WRITER,
SOULFUL LIFE & BUSINESS COACH.

Jaimsyne Blakely

Motivational Speaker, Writer, Soulful Life
& Business Coach.

California, United States

*"I believe in humanity; I believe in our individual
and collective ability to make the seemingly
impossible - possible."*

**What has driven you to create the success that you have?
(What is your WHY?)**

I am passionate about business being the place where ALL women
can bring ALL of their knowledge, wisdom, talents, skills, messy
brilliance, love, passion, mission and visions to the world.

I believe that it's important for women to rewrite the rules of business to
better support all of us. I acknowledge that women of all backgrounds
must be represented in business, and I take a stand for that, as it is
essential for us to care for ourselves, our families and communities,
and it is imperative in order for us to survive and thrive as a species.

Building a business online is the strongest and least expensive place
I know of where women can create community, acquire wealth, develop
our potential, increase our consciousness, share our talents and skills,
make an impact, and lead a revolution. I coach men and women on
how to do these things.

I believe in humanity; I believe in our individual and collective ability to
make the seemingly impossible - possible. I believe this is why humans
actually exist - to astound ourselves and each other with what we are
capable of creating.

We live in a time when we have many choices available to us: we
can get lost in information, stuck in transformation, or we can choose
the radical act of bringing something into the world that has never
previously existed. Every single business is a radical act of creation.

I was a business strategist, and I'm a four time start-up founder. I have
written many business plans for myself and for clients. I do not do that
anymore. Today, I know that All of the answers you and I need are
inside me and you. When I take the time to slow down, sit down, close
my eyes, look inside and place my focused attention and conscious
intention to ask for the next step, it is always revealed to me. I do this
everyday and I teach my clients how to do it, too.

When we take each step that comes from our internal guidance and repeat that process, every inspired action we need - to bring our desire or vision into reality - will be given. This is the Magic & Miracle Zone of life! We all have access to it, and when we practice it over and over, more of our human-spiritual Super Powers will be delivered to us. So we must use it!

I have been able to bring forth, create and actualize into the world the Divine Visions I see, the powerful and passionate Mission I feel, and the Rapture, Beauty and Shift in consciousness I receive. I coach my clients to do the same and I wish for everyone to experience it. I'm here to teach this! I am one of many who are taking a stand to support women and men to create soulful businesses.

If you were to choose 3 words that describe who you are as a woman, what would they be?
I AM Love; I AM Joy; I AM a Creator.

What role has vision boards and/or clearly defined goals played in your life and business?
This excellent question made me realize that I've been doing Vision Boards since I was a kid. I can see that I do them differently than I've noticed that most people do. Vision boards are so vital to my life that I work on mine every day.

I don't have goals anymore. I take the time to ask for and see the visions that are in me and I take very precise, very specific action steps toward realising my vision everyday.

I used to have many strategic S.M.A.R.T. goals and plans to achieve these. Rarely, did they happen as I desired, if at all.

Today, my actions are in alignment with my true desires. It's fun and far more productive to operate from my inner guidance.

Once I ditched my goals and began to do only what my guidance and my Visions directed me to actualize, my life opened up and I am now in the flow of joy nearly all the time.

My Vision boards used to be aspirational. For example, I "hoped" to bring to fruition each thing on my Vision Board (which I like to call my V Board). I do not hope anymore. Now, I know that I will actualize whatever I place my attention and intention upon because my Visions and Guidance come from God/Source within me.

I am actively in-creation on my V Boards every day. I have a different V Board for each Vision and project. I'm very visual, so words are like pictures to me, which is why many of my V Boards have more words and poetry than photos. I take time each day to calmly and open-heartedly sit with my Vision and let mySelf HEAR the Divine Guidance and SEE each next INspired action - and move as quickly as possible in FULL TRUST to accomplish each INspired action; rather than using my small, logical brain to strategize what it thinks each next step should be, thereby getting entangled in the details and having to slog through to completion.

By always working withIN, I know and trust that I'm in alignment with God/Source/The Divine. Goals seem very disconnected and external to me now. When I have a Vision, I know that God will give me each step to attain it. This is the wildly alive Magic & Miracles Zone I mentioned earlier.

How do you quieten the shame gremlins that say 'who do you think you are' or 'you're not enough'?

My antidote to this is to work from withIN. When I allow mySelf to sit with focused attention and conscious intention, my Divine Connection to Source/God is activated withIN me, then my Highest Self arises, and I see and hear the Divine Truth emerge.

There is no doubt or confusion in this place and space. When I create the time for myself to connect with Source within me, I am always rewarded with Divine clarity and guidance.

What does living a rich and prosperous life look like to you?

It means that I support mySelf to be all that I can be and to create what I envision. I am a multi-dimensional human.

Yes, I am a woman, yet I play many roles in my life. I have a conscious relationship with God, my Self, my body, mind, heart, spirit and Soul. I know that I am a Creator. I am a rememberer. I teach people to know who they are. My awareness of who I am and what I am capable of, my ability to see and understand others and comprehend what they are capable of, gives me the clarity and power to create whatever I desire. This feels rich!

Spending time and having SoulAdventures with my friends, family and clients. Doing work that I love: coaching, writing, creating soulful content, providing space for people to build an extraordinary business and live a gorgeous masterpiece of a life, meeting new people, spontaneous road trips on the highways and byways, challenging myself to deeper levels of communication with mySelf, my heart, body, mind, Spirit, Soul, Source, friends, family, clients, this all feels rich to me. My relationships are a huge part of my wealth.

I spent many years doing what I thought would support me financially, but those things didn't always light me up. It feels rich to be devoted to my own life Journey, to be in conscious creation of my own wealth, to teach others how to create and build wealth

I am continually developing a deeper relationship with my own consciousness. I spend time in deep connection with nature; make and share beautiful food at my table with friends, family, and clients (my social media is real!).

It feels rich to write for hours and share it! There's wealth spent in sharing time with friends and family while dancing, listening to music that someone plays from their heart and soul!

Camping, staying in beautiful hotels, listening to my friends play music, reading, watching movies, videos and art that moves me.

Reaching and expanding as I break free from old patterns and conditioning to clear mySelf, watching my clients become clear, seeing their lives change as they learn to unlock their Genius Code, and deepen their connection with Source and their Soul, discovering their passions, mission, vision and purpose, answering their callings, knowing who they truly are, having access to their human-spiritual Super Powers and learning to play with and create their visions big and small!

Loving people, people loving me, happy-surprising them, receiving happy surprises, living in the Magic & Miracles Zone, celebrating life and living full-out from withIN each day, the spiritual, mental and financial freedom to do whatever I desire, whenever I desire it, with whomever I desire, being in a constant love affair with mySelf and The Divine, experiencing the Divine's love for me.

Knowing that I am a Divine Creator and utilizing my human-spiritual ability to create anything my Soul desires and knowing that I can take the guided, INspired actions to co-create with God whatever I desire and more - this is how I live and this is my rich life!

Through your feminine lens, what does it mean to be a leader?

As a leader, I take 100% responsibility for my own outcomes, emotions, happiness, joy, health, well being, actions, results, choices, past, present and future. As a leader, I take a firm, bold stand for my work in the world, I support the craft of coaching and other brilliant coaches, I choose, share and uphold my own ethics, standards and boundaries in business and life.

I stand for my work in the world as a Creator, writer, filmmaker, videographer, coach, and happiness and human potential mentor.

I take a stand for what I believe in and know to be true. I Consciously work on mySelf through leadership exercises. I develop my talents and skills to more powerfully show up as a coach and loving presence of support to friends, family and the organizations I belong to.

I do the inner work to clear my Self of anything that might be a trigger so that I remain an advocate for my clients.

I support my own Visions and Mission. I work at being a raving fan of and cheerleader for my Self. I work at being an extraordinary wife, friend, daughter, sister, aunt, woman, coach, entrepreneur, writer, mentor, consultant, speaker. I work at keeping my heart open, being a student of life, love and business. I work at self-regulation and self-actualization, at expanding my heart, love, gratitude, wisdom.

I continually and consistently see the best in mySelf and push through my limitations and break through my stuckness to unleash more compassion toward mySelf and continually seek to blow my mind and exceed my understanding of what I'm capable of; I do the same thing for my clients.

I know WHO I am, WHY I'm here, and everyday I ask to know WHAT I'm being called to be, create, and cause. I work at being the fullest expression of my being, I work at respecting my time, my life and my talents. I am excited about fulfilling what God and I intend for me.

These are all the real steps I take to be in leadership of me, my life, my visions and my work.

What role has vulnerability played in your success story?

To me, vulnerability is the willingness and ability to express my full truth and to be fully present to hear the truth of another. In other words, vulnerability truly only happens when my heart is open to me, as well as to the other person. Vulnerability isn't a one way share. Real vulnerability is an intimate two-way experience; it's listening to yourSelf and the other, hearing what is said, and hearing what is not; it's being willing to be seen as you are in any given moment and to accepting the other as they are.

The role vulnerability plays in my success story is that as a Coach/daughter/sister/friend/partner/aunt/etc, I consciously commit to being present, curious, and open to hearing what my clients/friends/family have to say without first filtering it through my own experience and thereby misunderstanding their experience. I have done a lot of work in this area, so I am rarely triggered by or take personally what others say.

When I'm willing to fully share my truth and take responsibility for the consequences of sharing my truth, and I'm also willing to hear another person's truth fully, plus take 100% responsibility for my response to them sharing their truth, then I witness that my friends, family members and clients feel safe and this can give them a new freedom to express at a level that they might not ever have before and that often activates the courage within them to continue this as a life practice.

Whether being interviewed or interviewing others, what role have these connected conversations played in your business?

We all become more compassionate, interesting to others and intelligent through listening, we become more articulate, loving and expressive through sharing.

I learn who people are, what they've survived, how they've thrived, what holds them back, what lights them up, I learn more about mySelf, I discover unknown things and new ways of being through the art and practice of conscious, connected conversation.

Conscious, connected conversations are the foundation of my business and my life. Through these "explorations" of the soul, I learn, my clients learn, we emerge, grow and develop our trust in our Self, each other, our beloveds, God/Source and life itself. We come out of hiding, blossom, transcend out of old patterns and habits, and have more freedom to express, embody and be all that we are when we connect with another deeply.

When we experience the embodiment of trust at all 4 of these levels, we become whole. Without connected conversations, I would have no business and my clients and I would have no growth.

I have the deep relationships, friendships and freedom to express my deepest thoughts with my many beloved friends, family members, clients, colleagues, collaborators, partners and comrades because I practice deep connection. .

What is the most difficult decision you have had to make to pursue your dreams?

To pursue my dreams, I had to abandon my identity, leave my grandparents, my heroes, my benefactors of unconditional love, goodwill, verbal praise and emotional support. I had to leave home -before I was really ready - which was great practice for all of the things I've accomplished.

I had to let go of my connection to our farmland, the verdant green fields of alfalfa and clover, the memories yet to be made around my grandparent's spectacularly raucous, wildly fun, hysterically funny, comforting and delicious dinner table.

I had to leave the howls of the coyotes, the creaking of the willow tree, the mooing of the cows. I had to leave my beloved sisters, mom, aunts, uncles and cousins, my beautiful horses, my dog, the dozen barn cats, hundred or so chickens, couple hundred cattle, and the 47 raspberry bushes my Gramps planted just for me, the comforting silence, the yellow jackets, bumblebees and the sounds of nature in all her glory, the old tractor I learned to drive when I was 5, the miles of farm sprinklers, long country roads, helpful neighbors, fresh raw milk from our own cows, the smell of horse tack and fine leather saddles, the endless rides on horseback with my Gramps across nearby farms and into the pine-covered mountains that surrounded us, the blue-black sky with twinkling stars that reached out to forever and somehow circled back to hug you at night.

I knew I had to leave for the great unknown and say goodbye to my beloved Guardian Angels. Still, I have never forgotten how painful it was and how grateful I am for the memories and blessings afforded me by these generous, extraordinary Souls.

What are your core guiding values, and why?

Love - which is my compass, play - which is my North Star.

Intuition - which is my Wisdom and guides my way like a light.

Truth - because it really does set you free.

Courage - because that's where my confidence comes from.

Co-Creation - because consciously collaborating with God/Source is how we bring Heaven into earth/play our part to co-create Heaven on earth.

Divine GuiDANCE - because I KNOW each next INspired action step when I ask and when I step forth, I am always in Divine Alignment with Divine Timing.

SPICE - in my life, on my food, in what I create because it feels and tastes oh so delicious.

Soulfulness - because I'm more than a body, a mind, a heart and a Spirit - I am / you are a composite of all that ever was or will be in all of Creation.

These, too, are my core guiding values Miracles, Rapture, Wonder, Awe and Magic because these give us access to our human- spiritual Super Powers and they create the foundation for our ability to LIVE IN and BEcome our highest potential, JOY

- because well, it's joyFULL, exhilarating and awakening and I personally experience that this is the door to all Creation - SOUL ADVENTURE - because this is the path to actualizing everything - every single blissful thing - I desire.

What makes you come alive?

Being all in and playing full out with my life, my clients, and beloveds, loveLOVElove, NATURE, SOUL ADVENTURES, BEING A CREATOR, CREATING, BEING A WRITER, WRITING, CREATING BEAUTY, FEELING!!!! MUSIC, DANCING, SEX WITH MY BELOVED, MAKING HAPPY FOOD, SHARING KNOWLEDGE, KISSES & HUGS, TIME SPENT WITH MY NIECES & NEPHEWS, the ACT OF CREATION, the liberation of potential - my own and facilitating that for others, MAKING MAGIC, WORKING WONDERS, making SHIFT happen!

What self-love rituals do you prioritise and why?

Sitting with The Divine first thing each day and asking for my guiDANCE, DAILY Soul Adventures, bike riding at night with my hair flying behind me. Being on the beach and swimming like a mermaid. Working with aligned clients.

Time spent creating, writing, making movies and videos. Laughing, doing nothing, naps, chasing butterflies. Deep conversations with my friends, high-quality food and water. Wisdom walks in nature, learning something new to expand my heart.

Time with my body, mind, heart, Spirit and Soul, friends and family.

Learning new, amazing skills, riding horses, running, kayaking, and dancing with my hands in the air. Yoga, conscious connected breath-work, and making art.

Lovingly putting on clothes and jewelry that light me up and applying my make-up while happy-talking to my Self. Looking deeply into my Soul through my eyes to access my deepest truth, sitting with my pal, The Divine.

Making mySelf and my friends and family delicious, healthy food and serving it on my finest china.

Going barefoot, listening to my favorite music, taking a bath with rose petals, milk and honey surrounded by candles, talking with a friend, doing something meaningful and splendid for someone else.

What is your favourite strategy to unhook from procrastination?

Sit with God and dump everything in my head, heart and body onto the pages of a large art book and ask for SOULutions OR leave the house, take a SoulAdventure and ask that the answers to my questions be revealed along the way. The answers always come!

What would you say to the women who feel they should be able to do-it-all without a tribe/community/coach?

Stop being a lone Wolf! If you were a book, your Real Life would be found at the edges of your pages, not in the comfy center. If you are holding on to the notion that you're meant to do it alone, then you're stuck in the Lone Wolf paradigm.

It is crucial to our survival that women show up more powerfully in business; this is where we can impact our own lives and the lives of others.

Plus, it is elemental to our personal and collective happiness, joy, well being, health, wealth, family and bright futures to RECEIVE, not just give.

To be coached is to receive lavishly.

Let's acknowledge that we were all taught some crap about how to live, love and be successful. The whole notion of doing it alone doesn't really work. Success takes a tribe. Life and love require significant others.

When we are successful and happy on the inside, that clear, effervescent, light clarity will attract wondrous people, places, opportunities and invitations to us. We have the power within us to actualize anything we desire. Having a great coach in your corner helps you create faster and better.

The Divine is IN You. Everything you are is IN you. Find a Coach who speaks to your and Soul.

Take the leap to invest in yourSelf; YOU are the best investment YOU will ever have. YOU can go anywhere and actualize anything when you have your own back, are your own BFF, and ASK for support Trust. Ask, Listen. Receive. Prepare to be amazed!

Whose voices do you tune into for a guaranteed dose of inspiration?

The Divine. My own counsel. As for the voices of gorgeous others: Edwina Murphy-Droomer, Laura Hollick, Mary Oliver, David Whyte, Melanie Ann Layer, Stephanie Anne Hughson, Oprah, Rumi, Hafiz, John Randolph Price, The Rolling Stones, Aretha Franklin, Maya Angelou.

What role have coaches and/or masterminds played in your success?

I would not be as passionate, whole, loving, fierce, joyful, successful, clear, alive, and excited about life if it weren't for the extraordinary mentors I solicited to teach me, guide me, coach me.

The business consultants and coaches I've hired; the life coaches, financial coaches, food coach, health and wellbeing coach, eyesight coach, speaking coaches, vocal coaches (I used to sound like Minnie Mouse), vision coach (Edwina), film-making and video teachers and coaches, the 5 therapists. 3 psychologists, countless amazing shamans, Soul Shifters, the singing, acting and writing coaches, the 30-year marketing MasterMind and the various other MasterMinds I am in now and have been in have all greatly contributed to my success.

I would not be where I am without them.

Do you think you would be where you are now without having worked with a coach and why or why not?

It absolutely would not have been as fast, as fun and I would have missed out on what it's like to be seen, nurtured, held, nourished, supported, upheld, celebrated, challenged, and fiercely and lovingly confronted with my full permission.

What are you most grateful for?

I am most grateful to live in joyful co-creation in every part of my life with The Divine/Source/God.

What are your guilty pleasures?

Binge-watching the occasional South Korean TV series on Netflix (I loved Start Up)!

Shoes, shoes, shoes, did I say shoes?

The vegan Açaí Mousse at Erewhon market in Los Angeles!

Elemental raw food bars, I buy them by the case!

Dresses!

Luxury sheets!

Beautiful jewelry!

Spontaneous travel!

Mashed potatoes! Tacos! Smoothies!

Going out to breakfast, happy hour and dinner!

SoulAdventures!

What qualities do you see when you say, "She is a PHENOMENAL WOMAN!"?

After all the twists, turns, turbulence and tornadoes she's experienced in her life, she has come to love, adore and value herself - exactly as she is.

She is a little wild, elegant yet untamed, she's a straight shooter, loves deeply, is proud of herSelf for being non-judgemental of herSelf and others.

She listens, she cares; she is present, fun, can lovingly make fun of herself, is a good sport. She can read a room, knows when to take a stand, will not tolerate gossipers, knows how to take care of herSelf and has developed her talents, skills, strengths and abilities. She does not concern herself with what others think about her because she knows her worth and sees her value.

She has cultivated the ability to sustain joy, is comfortable in her skin, can articulate her thoughts, is aware of the feelings she's experiencing, is not wrapped up in her stories or the stories of others.

She does the work to lead her life. She takes 100% responsibility for her actions and lack of action, she knows she is a work in progress and is A-OK with that truth.

She trusts herself, others, God/Source and life itself. She likes her Self, loves herSelf,, knows what it means to be a good woman.

She is unapologetic in enforcing her boundaries because she knows the cost when she doesn't, she consciously creates and communicates new boundaries as needed.

She enjoys sharing pure expressions of her truth straight from her heart. She revels in her own power, laughs loudly, gives, and receives.

She loves to empower and celebrate other women to revel in their power and takes great pleasure in creating the space for other women to sparkle and shine.

She is honest with herSelf about what she wants. She celebrates her wins, can hold her power and manage her energy.

She honors her word, is accomplished at not taking things personally, does not expect perfection of herself or others, is kind to her people and all people.

She celebrates the work of others, is open to new things and experiences. She encourages, inspires and glitters with her integrity, alignment, truth and wisdom. She values her mind, body, heart, Spirit and Soul!

She is a Phenomenal Woman!

Jaimsyne Blakely Links

 instagram.com/JaimsyneBlakely   youtube.com/JaimsyneBlakely   🌐 www.Jaimsyne.com

📘 facebook.com/JaimsyneBlakely   🐦 twitter.com/JaimsyneBlakely

Chelsea Clarke

CONTENT MONETIZATION STRATEGIST
AND WEBSITE INVESTOR. FOUNDER
OF HERPAPERROUTE.

Chelsea Clarke

Content Monetization Strategist and
website investor. Founder of HERPAPERROUTE.

British Columbia, United States

*"I will never forget how miserable I was as an
employee, and I don't take it for granted one
moment now that I get to work from home, happy,
completely on my own terms doing what I love."*

**What has driven you to create the success that you have?
(What is your WHY?)**

It is a combination of a few factors. One big reason why I am driven
in my career as an entrepreneur now is that I truly hated being an
employee and will never forget the struggle.

My first job was at 12 years old, and I had after school, weekend and
Summer jobs until I finished University, and then went straight into the
workforce full-time until I was 30. Usually working two full-time jobs at
once, on top of various online side hustles. It was a lot!

There isn't one thing I liked about working for someone else. From
having to sell my time to make someone else rich, to having to leave
the house. It was all a huge detriment to my own business success
and my happiness. So when I finally decided to quit all of my jobs and
side-hustles and go full-on in my own business (I'm a website investor),
everything finally made sense. I will never forget how miserable I was
as an employee, and I don't take it for granted one moment now that
I get to work from home, happy, completely on my own terms doing
what I love. I just wish I didn't wait until I was 30 to leap!

Another reason why I am driven is that it is important to me that I
provide for my family and show my son what's possible when you
follow your own path. On a personal level, it's a rush whenever I close
a $100,000 deal or sell a site for a huge profit. It's addictive but in a
good way!

If you were to choose 3 words that describe who you are as a woman, what would they be?

I am independent, focused and resourceful.

These traits (or perhaps learned skills) have helped me on my journey in business. Being independent has allowed me the free will and confidence to do what I've wanted to do without hesitation. I get an idea, and I start implementing it. If I want to invest in something or make a decision, I do it without the need for anyone else's input or permission.

What role has vision boards and/or clearly defined goals played in your life and business?

I believe that having clearly defined goals is incredibly important in life and business. Without something to work towards, the days will go by with no results, and we won't get ahead. I'm not fancy about it - I just write out my goals on a piece of paper and take note when I hit certain milestones on the road to achieving them. Seeing your goals written out and seeing them often is an important element in the overall plan. We need to be reminded of the things we are working towards, and we need to feel that validation when we cross it off the list when completed.

A few years back, my husband and I had a brain dump and wrote everything we wanted to do. From small, fun things like "Get matching tattoos", "Get an espresso machine", "Go to one of those gyms full of trampolines", to the more grand goals "buy a house", "start a family", "save $200,000."

It was a huge list with over 100 goals on it. At the time, we were living in a small apartment, had little savings, and each made just enough to get by at our jobs. We kept the list on our fridge and slowly started crossing off goals. By the next year, we had crossed off all the small goals and most of the big goals too!

We were approved for a mortgage to buy our first place, started our own businesses, made weekly payments towards our savings goal, and the baby was on the way. Oh, and we had those matching tattoos, too!

Clearly defined goals and objectives have allowed me to track and monitor my progress as a business owner, too. It is important to have both short and long term goals that are specific, measurable, attainable, relevant and time-based. Better known as "S.M.A.R.T. Goals". Goal setting provides me with direction, a clearer focus and clarity in decision making when it comes to my business and personal life.

How do you quieten the shame gremlins that say 'who do you think you are' or 'you're not enough'?

Imposter syndrome is a sneaky dream-zapper. It's that voice that creeps up and tells you that you aren't qualified or educated enough. Usually, it appears right when you are about to try something new or are about to push yourself out of your comfort zone. It wants to sabotage you and keep you small. Here's the thing - it's very common to hear the voice of imposter syndrome. But it is your duty to ignore it. Push that voice down, tell that little jerk to take a hike, and then continue doing what you wanted to do, how you wanted to do it. Imposter syndrome doesn't necessarily go away (even when you are super successful!); you will just get better at ignoring it. That's the key.

What does living a rich and prosperous life look like to you?

To live a rich and prosperous life is to find a balance of the most important things to you. For me, that is my family and my work. Prosperity is essential for having the tools to achieve your goals in life, which is why it was so important for me to climb out of debt after I was laid off from my corporate marketing job.

Happiness is a state of mind that comes from being your authentic self and committing to a life of health and wellness. Every day I live my life and run my business consistent with my beliefs and values, so I know that my successes are aligned with my passions.

But I didn't always have this positive outlook.

In the past 10 years, I have done a complete 180 on the old, problematic money mindset of my youth. When I was growing up, I was taught (indirectly) that money is bad. I overheard my family speak about money throughout my childhood - their lack of it and everyone else's abundance of it - as a terrible, stressful thing. Because of this, without meaning to, I grew up subconsciously thinking that If you have lots of money, you must be greedy, just lucky, or did something nefarious. If you drive a nice car, you are showing off or trying to overcompensate for personal shortcomings. If you go on vacations or save for your children's college, you are somehow out of touch with reality and continue a cycle of greed and laziness. Ouch!

Yes, part of my having these bad mindset beliefs was how my family spoke about money. But it was also a result of my own experience as a broke college student who had to work two jobs to afford to pay my tuition and rent, usually couldn't afford to buy groceries, and had to go to the food bank. I was burnt out and jealous of my friend's whose parents paid their tuition, rent, food, and even bought them cars!

It wasn't until my late 20s when I finally realized that money, wealth, and success are actually good things to strive for. And that when you have money, you can have a bigger impact on the world and help more people. The point of having lots of money is so that you can afford yourself the lifestyle freedom to do what you really want. To spend your time with your loved ones and make changes in the world that matter to you.

I had to do some internal work on myself to figure this out, and break the cycle of my own past, damaging beliefs about money and success - and it feels awesome on the other side now!

Nowadays, living rich and prosperous is about having the freedom to spend time with my family, knowing that we are saving for our futures and our children's education without spending a minute of our time working for someone else. Being able to invest and see our money grow for generational wealth while donating to the causes we care about is living rich and prosperous to me!

Through your feminine lens, what does it mean to be a leader?

A leader is someone who can do it all but knows not to. A leader delegates to her team to focus her attention on the most important, money-generating tasks, trusting that her team has everything else under control. A leader supports her team through honest feedback and encouragement. She gives credit to those who create and knows not to blame anyone but herself when she makes an error.

To be a leader is to help guide others to success based on your own personal experiences, whether that be your successes or failures. Everything that I encounter as an entrepreneur counts as a learning experience going forward. So, to be a leader in my industry is to share my knowledge with others and help guide them towards success.

What is the most difficult decision you have had to make to pursue your dreams?

The most difficult decision felt impossible before it was made. But then, once I made the decision, I realized it was the easiest thing ever and that I should have made it a decade ago. And that was to decide to believe in me and quit my job to focus on starting my own business.

Before I took the leap, I was worried about the unknown. But the moment I walked out of those office doors that last time, every feeling of uncertainty washed away and was replaced by a tsunami of excitement for what I now had the time to finally begin.

What is your favourite strategy to unhook from procrastination?

More often than not, procrastination is perceived as laziness, when in reality, procrastination is a combination of negative emotions like stress, boredom or anxiety. I wish there were magic medicine that could solve procrastination, but I have a few tips and tricks that have helped me in the past.

Instead of catastrophizing the task at hand, I try to break it up into smaller pieces that are more manageable to look at. Then, I get out my planner and calendar and give myself deadlines to complete what I need. The best way to get over procrastination is just to begin.

On the other end of the spectrum, it is sometimes helpful for me to completely step away from the task at hand and focus on something else. It can be so easy to hyper fixate on your work and lose your creativity and drive. Taking time away from my computer and having a meal with my family, taking a walk, or watching an episode of my favorite TV show usually helps me give my mind a break and refocus.

When I am feeling detached from a responsibility and catch myself pushing tasks closer to a deadline, it's a sign that I need a change of perspective to clear my head. So I will remove myself from the project for a day, take a walk, run around outside with my kid/dog, and just do something completely away from my computer. Sometimes I'll spend an hour doing something a little mindless, like watching reality TV. This helps me to just unwind, chill and reframe my attention away from the grind of work.

Then when I return to my computer screen, later on, I'll feel refreshed and ready to turn my brain back on and tackle the job.

Something that I started doing a year ago is each quarter; I will book myself into a hotel and spend a few days just working and creating, without any distractions or interruptions.

As a work from home mom who usually works while her kid does backflips around her, these little solo hotel work-cations are awesome. It really helps me plan my company's next quarter, tackle projects with loose ends, and create content.

What would you say to the women who feel they should be able to do-it-all without a tribe/community/coach?

Well, I would say you can do it all yourself. But why? Just because you are an entrepreneur doesn't mean you should be a lone wolf. Truthfully, there are people who can help get you to the next step a lot faster. Hire a team, work with a mentor, network and make business buddies in your industry. Being a part of a community in your industry can be wonderful and open up many doors. For example, I have made incredible connections through networking, which has led me to be invited to speak in summits, share stages, co-host workshops and more. Opportunities I would never have been offered had I kept to myself and not put myself out there in my industry.

I would tell do-it-all women that there is no shame in asking for help. Rather it shows strength to seek knowledge and advice from others. So, get out there and let the world know what you do. Make that hire, sign that coach, make that introduction.

Whose voice/s do you tune into for a guaranteed dose of inspiration?

Jen Sincero (author of the 'You Are A Badass' books) is one of the funniest, no-BS, brilliant people around. I seek out all the podcasts she appears on whenever I need a dose of inspiration. Another inspiring badass woman is Cher. I love the story of when Cher's mom advised her to marry a rich man, and Cher's response was, "But mom, I am a rich man." I live by those words!

What are you most grateful for?

I am grateful for so much; it's hard to pick one thing. Yes, that sounds cheesy, but I mean that every big good thing we have is happening due to hundreds of little good and bad things that happened and led to it.

I am grateful for the health and happiness of my family. I'm grateful that I wandered into that random bar in 2015 where I met the guy who I'd marry. I'm grateful that we eloped a month later, even when our friends and families warned us not to - we knew what we were doing!

I'm grateful that I opened Facebook that day to see an ad for a virtual summit for creators, as what I learned by attending that event led me to launch my business with confidence. I'm equally as grateful for the day that I opened Facebook to see a post about a rescue dog who needed a home - I can't imagine what life was like before that dog joined our family! I used to hold aggression towards my Dad for leaving us when I was a baby and never being in my life (and still isn't). But I've since let go of that anger, and I am even grateful for him because of his part in bringing me into this beautiful life. How's that for cheese? :)

What qualities do you see when you say, "She is a PHENOMENAL WOMAN!"?

Every woman is phenomenal. Every woman has her own strengths, abilities and gifts. But someone confident in her ability to be herself, take charge, live her life how she sees fit, doesn't ask for permission, or depend on anyone else for her own financial and lifestyle freedom is phenomenal in my books.

There are so many traits of so many different women that make them phenomenal. If I were to boil it down into just a few things, they would be strong-willed, independent and compassionate. Society tries to put women in a box, and it is so important to be unapologetically yourself and do what you want even if others advise against it. I say independent because being financially independent and self-sustained when it comes to finances is an incredibly important experience to reach.

Lastly, I believe that compassion is what makes us good, kind, loving people. Compassion for people, animals and yourself should always be of the highest priority, and anyone who demonstrates this is phenomenal. This is obviously not an all-inclusive list of what makes a woman phenomenal, but this begins to explain my own definition of what I feel is phenomenal.

Chelsea Clarke Links

instagram.com/herpaperroute

facebook.com/groups/herpaperroute

youtube.com/herpaperroute

twitter.com/herpaperroute

www.herpaperroute.com

Sarah Louise

AUTHOR, LIFE COACH,
SPEAKER, HEALER AND
LIGHT WORKER.

Sarah Louise

Author, life coach, speaker, healer and light worker.

Queensland, Australia

"Without creating goals and a clear vision, I get totally lost, unfocused and unmotivated. I am always working on creating clear visions in pursuit of my next goal."

What has driven you to create the success that you have? (What is your WHY?)
I have always followed my passion for helping others; my success has come as a by-product of following my passion.

If you were to choose 3 words that describe who you are as a woman, what would they be?
Aware, Authentic, Magic

What role have vision boards and/or clearly defined goals played in your life and business?
HUGE!! Without creating goals and a clear vision, I get totally lost, unfocused and unmotivated. I am always working on creating clear visions in pursuit of my next goal.

How do you quieten the shame gremlins that say 'who do you think you are' or 'you're not enough'?
I remember how far I have come and the lessons I have gone through to get to today; that makes me feel like I deserve the world and I am enough.

What does living a rich and prosperous life look like to you?
Living in the flow, aware and conscious, knowing I have everything I want and need and that life always works out for me. Seeing my loved ones happy and healthy living their dreams.

Through your feminine lens, what does it mean to be a leader?
To practice what you preach and walk and talk your message in an authentic way.

What role has vulnerability played in your success story?
100% of the role

Whether being interviewed or interviewing others, what role have these connected conversations played in your business?

Being interviewed has been a great way to share my message, collaborate with others, and share with a greater community.

What is the most difficult decision you have had to make to pursue your dreams?

I left a marriage.

What are your core guiding values, and why?

Love – It's the only thing that matters.
Health – It's the basis of how I feel.
Connection – It's my purpose.

What makes you come alive?

Teaching and inspiring others how they can live happily ever after

What self-love rituals do you prioritise and why?

Looking after me is high on my priorities as I know how important self-love and self-care is. I book a massage usually weekly in a beautiful local spa, and I relish the experience every time—the tea, the smells, the bliss of it all.

What is your favourite strategy to unhook from procrastination?

Usually, go for a walk or listen to something motivational.

What would you say to the women who feel they should be able to do-it-all without a tribe/community/coach?

You can always do it alone, but it's incredible to walk together, to feel supported, understood and seen and heard; as Women, it's what we need to grow.

Whose voices do you tune into for a guaranteed dose of inspiration.

I'm a real Ester Hicks fan; I have been since I was 18! I also love some David Goggin's if I need to get motivated.

What role have coaches and/or masterminds played in your success?

I have always had coaches and therapists to help me believe in myself to keep stepping up in life. They have played a monumental part in my life; without their love, guidance and support, I would never be where I am today,

Do you think you would be where you are now without having worked with a coach and why or why not?

No, I would never have understood myself and life with the outside help of others.

What are you most grateful for?

My awareness and connection to life.

What are your guilty pleasures?

Roses and chocolate.

What qualities do you see when you say, "She is a PHENOMENAL WOMAN!"?

Authentic, Inspirational, Compassionate, Confident, Resilient & Ambitious.

Sarah Louise Links

📷 instagram.com/sarahlouiselive

📘 facebook.com/SarahLouiseLeaderInLight

🌐 www.sarahlouise.live

Authentic,
Inspirational,
Compassionate,
Confident,
Resilient &
Ambitious.

SARAH LOUISE

Dr Izdihar Jamil Ph.D.

BUSINESS COACH AND #1 INTERNATIONAL BESTSELLING AUTHOR.

Dr Izdihar Jamil, Ph.D.

Business Coach and #1 International
Bestselling Author.

California, United States

*"I chose to trust myself and surround myself with
people who will support me to take action. My key
is to keep moving forward one day at a time, and
success will be my destiny."*

**What has driven you to create the success that you have?
(What is your WHY?)**

When I came to America to support my husband with his dream job,
I left a secured position and my family behind. I had 2 young children,
and I knew I didn't want to go back to a 9-5 job. I knew that I always
had something more within me. I crave FREEDOM. Freedom of time,
money, choices, physicality. I wanted to create my own rules and
success while looking after my family.

Also, when we first got to America, we were verbally harassed due to
our faith and beliefs. It made me scared to go out and thought that I had
made the biggest mistake by coming to America. One day while I was
reading a storybook to my kids, I came across one line. I felt that God
was directly speaking to me, and at that moment, I knew that everything
would be OK.

At that moment, I chose to shift my mindset. With my husband's support
by purchasing an online business course for me, I chose to focus on
helping people and building a successful business online. I have never
looked back. The event that happened, coupled with my desire for
freedom, the feeling that there's "always more" of me, my family and
helping other women are the core of my success.

**If you were! to choose 3 words that describe who you are as a
woman, what would they be?**

Loving, Happy, Unstoppable

What role has vision boards and/or clearly defined goals played in your life and business?

Every week I would email myself 10-15 goals. It helped me to be focused on what really matters. I'm really thankful to say that each of those goals has been manifested. For those that haven't, I trust that it will come at a Divine timing.

How do you quieten the shame gremlins that say 'who do you think you are' or 'you're not enough'?

They would always be there, especially when I'm up levelling myself. I chose to trust myself and surround myself with people who will support me to take action. My key is to keep moving forward one day at a time, and success will be my destiny.

What does living a rich and prosperous life look like to you?

Me hanging out with my family and not having to do any housework. I get to travel to see my Mom and Dad in Malaysia at any moment that I choose. Once a year, I would host a retreat at the most beautiful island in the world with other female entrepreneurs to recharge our business and health. I am able to retire myself and my husband. I get to bake and read at any time I please. I get to buy things without looking at the price tag. I get to contribute to my community and other women with my skills and experience.

Through your feminine lens, what does it mean to be a leader?

Someone who is loving, compassionate, visionary and unstoppable. Success as a wife, mother and business owner is non-negotiable—the ability to do minimum work with maximum results.

What role has vulnerability played in your success story?

It made me relatable to others. It made me realise that on the other side of my vulnerability is my greatest key to success.

Whether being interviewed or interviewing others, what role have these connected conversations played in your business?

To be highly visible by reaching out to thousands and thousands of people. It also solidified my status as the #1 Authority in my field. It's one of my lead generation tools while connecting with the interviewer and his/her audience. Most importantly, my voice is heard, and I pray that it'll help shine the light on others.

What is the most difficult decision you have had to make to pursue your dreams?

To break through my own glass ceiling and self-limiting beliefs and know that there's always more of me. For example, when I was first offered the opportunity to appear on Forbes, I was scared. I said, "Forbes isn't looking for someone like me". With some nurturing, an amazing lady told me that "What are you talking about? You're hot property!". The moment I chose to shift my mindset and embrace that I'm hot property to be featured on Forbes, things shifted. A few weeks later, I had a FULL feature on Forbes, one of the most iconic brands in the world.

What are your core guiding values, and why?

Doing something that God will be pleased with me. My family, Freedom in all areas of life. The ability to create new things and to have fun doing it.

What makes you come alive?

When I experience heartfelt love. Loving myself and being loved by others. Freedom in all areas of my life, money, choices, people, lifestyle, makes me feel that I could fly so high and nothing could stop me—the ability to have fun creating new things in my life and business.

What self-love rituals do you prioritise and why?

Reading, baking and giving myself a facial. When I give myself ME and prioritise ME, I feel so happy because, with 3 kids, I can easily become drained if I don't look after myself.

What is your favourite strategy to unhook from procrastination?

Keep things simple. Just do one thing. A step a day helps me to move forward until one day it is done! Simple is ca$h.

What would you say to the women who feel they should be able to do-it-all without a tribe/community/coach?

Why go through all the pain and suffering? Why not allow yourself a shortcut? Smart women know how to leverage.

When I was at the lowest of low, an amazing woman picked me up, and I will never forget that. I am here because of my family, coaches, friends and community.

Whose voices do you tune into for a guaranteed dose of inspiration?

Victoria Beckham, Vanessa Ogden Moss, Jack Cranfield, Grant Cardone, Ken Honda, Brian Tracy.

What role have coaches and/or masterminds played in your success?

It made things easy for me to follow in their footsteps. It gave me the love, support and confidence that I need to move forward. I don't have time for complicated stuff. I love having access to shortcuts because I know I can fast track my success.

Do you think you would be where you are now without having worked with a coach and why or why not?

Maybe. But what I do know is that it has helped accelerate my success with little pain and suffering.

What are you most grateful for?

My family, my support system, my friends and my courage for making things happen.

What are your guilty pleasures?

I could literally binge on Netflix and reading books all day long!

What qualities do you see when you say, "She is a PHENOMENAL WOMAN!"?

Love, grace, happiness and unstoppable. :)

Dr Izdihar Jamil Links

instagram.com/izdiharjamil

facebook.com/izdihar.jamil.1

www.izdiharjamil.com

twitter.com/IzdiharJamil

Meredith Allan

KEYNOTE SPEAKER, TV HOST, SMART
MARKETING EXPERT FOUND ON NBC,
CBS, FOX, ABC & CNN.

Meredith Allan

Keynote Speaker, TV Host, Smart Marketing
Expert found on NBC, CBS, FOX, ABC & CNN.

California, United States

"When I let go of 'pretending everything was perfect', so much fun bubbled up in my life. That's where the connection is. I believe when people let go, they learn to connect deeply."

What has driven you to create the success that you have? (What is your WHY?)

Because I was not born into privilege, I have always been inspired by my parents about what is possible, despite the odds. Through the years, I've been influenced not only by my mother's optimism and my father's humor, but really, they've always instilled in me that my dreams are important, and they are possible. Making dreams possible (even against the odds) is my 'why' for everything that I do. It is my inspiration, as I mentor people all over the world, and is my inspiration every time I hit a stage and have the honor of lifting or leading an audience to limitless possibilities.

If you were to choose 3 words that describe who you are as a woman, what would they be?

Loving, courageous and powerful.

What role has vision boards and/or clearly defined goals played in your life and business?

I believe that vision boards and clearly defined goals literally make or break a dream come true. I was so fortunate that at the age of 14, I had the pleasure of hearing a speaker say that less than 1% of the world sets goals. So if you set goals for your dreams, you are 99% ahead of the rest of the world. And once I heard that it was like something ignited inside me. I broke many records by becoming the first in my family to receive multiple scholarships to college and the first to receive awards for working for more television stations than any other student had during my time in college.

I then went on to work for one of the world's most famous journalists. Many young people don't know the name now, but Barbara Walters was a big deal when I was younger. She was the first woman in broadcasting to ever land a major network gig as an anchorwoman in the United States; this inspired me a great deal. Having a vision board connected me every day with laser clarity to my dream life and moved me forward faster.

How do you quiet the shame gremlins that say 'who do you think you are' or 'you're not enough'?

I've never had a "you're not enough" problem with confidence. My loving parents told me from a young age that I could be president of anything if I set my mind to it. I have endured being the target of jealousy from others.

My mother explained that when people are mean to you or tell you things aren't possible, it is not my concern. Over the years, I have noticed when people are nasty or spiteful; it is often rooted in their own insecurity. I have learned to do my best never to take things personally. I believe we should be so busy improving ourselves we shouldn't have time to think about other opinions.

I grew up confident that all my dreams were possible. I learned from a young age that arrogance is not admirable and to do my best to be kind, happy, and powerful.

What does living a rich and prosperous life look like to you?

Living a rich and prosperous life means living in freedom and on my terms. For a long time, as a younger lady, I sold out. I believed that working for somebody else was the only path and something that I just had to suffer through. For many years I really did suffer working in television. I worked horrific hours doing overnights and early mornings.

I worked every holiday for more than a decade, including Christmas and Thanksgiving, as that's what I was told you had to do to get ahead. I was told to give work 110% by my parents, who did not have things handed to them. Growing up and not being in privilege meant that we were to work as hard as possible, as often as possible, to achieve whatever is possible. And now, I'm very excited to be in my 40s with a very different belief system.

I believe being rich in health is truly wealth and being surrounded by family and friends is everything. These days I live my dreams, overlooking a spectacular view, watching sailboats head out for sunset cruises right outside my window. This was my dream for a very long time, and it seemed unattainable in many moments, too expensive and too far fetched. So, for me being rich is going forward, no matter what odds are stacked against you or how loud the voices of others who doubt you are, going forward towards your dream is living a rich and prosperous life.

I've noticed that when we live a life in service, fulfilling dreams, lifting others high and leading others to fulfill their dreams, it feels very abundant, and the money does flow. So I've learned it's when I hold myself back, when I'm restrictive, when I am afraid to surrender, that's what gets in the way of success.

Through your feminine lens, what does it mean to be a leader?

I don't often think in terms of masculine and feminine. So this is fun to consider...

I think being a leader is not letting somebody else define us and, at times, being willing to stand up and say, "This isn't right", when no one else will. I also believe in being a loving interruption and being willing to say hard things people may not want to hear but need to hear. I have noticed that many people shy away from difficult conversations, and I'm not one of those people. I learned long ago, perhaps from my mother, who was quite a role model for me, that we don't have to have live a stereotypical "stay at home, homemaker life".

Leadership is whatever you choose to make it; it could be leading your family, leading a corporation, leading the Parent-Teacher Association. I'm doing my best to lead my company and family and to do it with grace.

I pride myself in being the kind of leader who doesn't freak out under pressure but rather is wise enough to lead with grace, generosity and kindness. That's true leadership to me.

Being a leader is being willing to go places that nobody else will go, being willing to say things that nobody else will say, and being willing to love on another level. And what I mean by that is, you've got to love yourself a lot, to push through fear. I take pride in having Edwina Murphy-Droomer as a true friend and being willing to see what is possible through the eyes of each other when we are struggling to see it for ourselves. True leadership is being strong enough to know that we don't have to struggle alone, we don't have to hide, and we get to be supported in life.

What role has vulnerability played in your success story?

Vulnerability and being willing to share my pain openly has unlocked all of the greatest joys in my life. One of the greatest moments I had was sharing a stage with Edwina, where we were both acknowledged for creating phenomenal success in just 12 months. When sharing my story, I decided to be very vulnerable about the challenges I had faced. I talked about being blindsided when my father was diagnosed with terminal cancer and how hard it was to find the strength to keep going. As a result, I gained several clients that day because, they later told me, they admired how brave and honest I was about my journey to success.

Watching my father die very quickly and horrifically suffering from pancreatic cancer changed me forever. I think that story resonates with so many people because unexpected changes are coming for all of us. Some of us choose to power through tough times; however, in my experience, this does not work well, as the pain can take us by surprise if we try to stuff it away. Having spent years as a workaholic obsessed with getting promotions or future vacations. Now I believe living in the moment and being present to all the joy and gifts each day delivers is the best way to live our lives. I no longer work weekends and do my best to disconnect from electronics sundown Fridays to Saturdays.

Though I never saw it coming, losing my father to cancer up-levelled my strength, resilience, and capacity to love. His legacy lives on with my love and generosity and the understanding that being loving and kind is the most important gift we can give others. Leading with love is the greatest vulnerable lesson of my life.

Whether being interviewed or interviewing others, what role have these connected conversations played in your business?

Being interviewed and interviewing others as a journalist has been a game-changer. Whether I'm live on Facebook or on stage or sharing via my blog, my fans connect deeply with me. I have this ability to disarm people with the truth, with a laugh, and by just showing up raw and real. And I wasn't always that way. But when I really found the courage to 'lift the veil' and let my guard down, my career really took off. As a TV personality, I had to have perfect hair and smile, smile, smile! When I let go of "pretending everything was perfect", so much fun bubbled up in my life. That's where the connection is. I believe when people let go, they learn to connect deeply.

People don't hire me just because I'm a marketing expert or someone who can help you master your message; I believe I'm hired time and time again because of my willingness to be real.

Because I'm not afraid to open up and be really honest and real about my wins and my mistakes.

I think these are the things that define us, and we don't need to be ashamed of them.

Words are just such beautiful things. And that's how I've made my living, connecting as a journalist through peoples stories, the messy and the magnificent.

What is the most difficult decision you have had to make to pursue your dreams?

Moving across the country, along an uncharted course, alone with my dog, driving over 3000 miles after selling or donating everything that I owned. Ironically, out of every possession that I gave away or sold, the one thing I cried over was my paddle board. Now, I have unlimited access to paddle boards, but you know, we all have our attachments to things, and as I've gotten older, I've just felt less and less attached to things and more attached to being brave and willing to do whatever it takes to live my dream.

I haven't regretted that brave move for a moment. It hasn't been easy, but as soon as I made up my mind to go for it, amazing magical, beautiful things came into my life. The decision to commit to my dream was more important than sitting in fear, pausing, wishing, wanting and hoping.

I have no regrets. The magic is in being willing to go for it. Even if you don't have it all figured out. Even if you haven't a clue how you're going to get there, just being brave enough to say, today, I'm going to take a step and then taking another, and then the next day taking another.

What are your core guiding values, and why?

My core guiding values are integrity, loyalty, being loving and generous. As a Kabbalist, I follow Kabbalah, so the most defining thing in my life is showing up in every situation with, "How can I be the light? How can I be the light to my friends? How can I be the light to my sweet dog Biscuit? How can I be the light to an audience? How can I be the light to my mother?"

And another value that has changed the course of my life is the choice to be proactive rather than reactive in life.

I think most of the world runs around having things happen and reacting. It's quite natural; actually, it's more unnatural to pause and be so clear about how you want to respond. Somebody could be cursing at you, or somebody could cut you off in traffic, and you could STILL choose to be kind and loving and think, "I hope they're okay. It's not about me, I don't need to take it personally, and I don't need to react".

And every time I choose to be loving in those trying moments, I feel it's a win. It's a win for the person receiving my love and light. Life isn't about what people are giving you. It's about how you show up anyway.

What makes you come alive?

What makes me come alive is inspiring others, knowing I'm making a difference. Always choosing kindness makes me feel so good and being generous in all ways whenever possible.

What self-love rituals do you prioritise and why?

My self-love rituals include lots of baths, giggle fests with my best friends, and making time for meditation to quieten my mind, body and soul, and doing yoga. I have also fallen in love with running again in my 40s and am lifting weights. It feels so good to live the best life I can whilst being the healthiest I've ever been.

What is your favourite strategy to unhook from procrastination?

My favourite strategy to unhook procrastination is to have a coach and an accountability partner. In truth, my entire life, I've battled it. Some people just function better at the last minute. I'm answering the call to be a part of this book at the very last minute. I might be the very last submission. And it's not for any lack of love for the project. It's a habit I always work to break.

Procrastination is not something I advise, but if you find yourself a creative person like me, who is sometimes on her own timetable, I think it's best to allow your friends to call you forward and really realise that we all get to receive support. For all these reasons, I believe coaching is awesome.

What would you say to the women who feel they should be able to do-it-all without a tribe/community/coach?

I don't believe in doing it all, period. Women who feel they should be able to do it all are subscribing to a myth. I think a tribe, community, or coach will always be the answer to push you forward, and ideally, I believe we would all benefit from having all three.

Whose voices do you tune into for a guaranteed dose of inspiration?

My greatest inspirations are a mixture of Les Brown and TD Jakes. This is funny as TD Jakes is a Christian minister, and I am a Jewish girl from the suburbs of Philadelphia, but what I love about TD Jakes and Les Brown is their passion.

I also love listening to Abraham Hicks and Lisa Nichols, who is my favorite public speaker of all time.

And, of course, my friends and family are also a tremendous source of inspiration.

What role have coaches and/or masterminds played in your success?

Masterminds and coaches have literally altered the course of my life. I run a mastermind, and I am a coach. I know that without a community and a coach, you can move forward but not as fast.

Do you think you would be where you are now without having worked with a coach and why or why not?

I believe that it is human nature to live in mediocrity. And once I discovered that there are people out there who strive to do everything with excellence, integrity, and heart, I knew those were my people.

The idea that we can always transform, we can always level up, lights up my heart.

I don't think you can do that by yourself. You cannot transform without support. If you want to level up your business or life, you get to have a coach; you get to have a mentor; you get to have a community. When you have all of those things, you will alter the course of your life in a beautiful way.

What are you most grateful for?

I'm most grateful for the bumps in the road. I know that sounds unusual, but I've learned who I am through adversity.
I once heard Marsha Weider say, " love your wounds". I thought that was the weirdest, wackiest, West Coast concept. And now I live here, and I guess I just get it.

The truth is, if life is all sunshine and roses, we wouldn't appreciate it. It's being knocked down and getting up again that creates gratitude. It's the things that I didn't see coming that I'm so grateful for now as they have redefined what I now see as important.

What are your guilty pleasures?

I like to binge-watch Netflix. I'm currently watching Ozark. I'm actually watching several shows at once, and I'm reading something like six books at once. I think it's a fun way to escape. Also, I love a pajama day, having girls spa days and massages. Those are some of my guilty pleasures.

What qualities do you see when you say, "She is a PHENOMENAL WOMAN!"?

A Phenomenal Woman is a woman who lives in grace, generosity, courage and kindness.

Meredith Allan Links

ⓞ *instagram.com/themeredithshow*

f *facebook.com/TheMeredithShow*

🐦 *twitter.com/mediameredth*

🌐 *www.themeredithshow.com/*

Elizabeth de Moraes

SUCCESS & MEDIA PRESENCE
COACH, CREATOR OF THE VIDEO
GLAM CAM KIT® PRODUCTS.

Elizabeth de Moraes,
M.A., M.F.A.

Success & Media Presence Coach,
Creator of The Video Glam Cam Kit® Products.

Texas, United States

"Writing my goals down as well as putting them on a vision board have been paramount in the success in my business."

What has driven you to create the success that you have? (What is your WHY?)

All my life, I have been driven to make an impact to leave a mark, to change people's lives and help them see life in a different way that is full of opportunity, and possibility.

I understand that when an idea or a dream is seated in our heart, we are meant to fulfill it. As a result, I have an insatiable desire to fulfill what I came here to be.

Another big part of my Why are our girls who are 17 and 12. I want them to know that their mom did everything that she could to be a full expression of who she is. It is also important to me to leave them with guidance and a blueprint, or at least an example of what they can do with their lives.

If you were to choose 3 words that describe who you are as a woman, what would they be?

Courageous, creative, and caring.

What role has vision boards and/or clearly defined goals played in your life and business?

Writing my goals down as well as putting them on a vision board have been paramount in the success in my business.

I just recently went through a group of my notes of goals and folded up vision boards from the past, and in that pile, I was astonished to find just how many of those goals have been fulfilled and are now just everyday life for me.

When we have a clear vision placed in front of us on a daily basis, we are reminded of it and are more likely to take the actions that will bring the vision into reality. If not, life happens, they are easily forgotten, with our goals less likely to be attained.

How do you quieten the shame gremlins that say 'who do you think you are' or 'you're not enough'?

This is something that I've dealt with and sometimes still deal with a lot over the years. From early childhood and throughout our lives, we sign contracts with ourselves, both positive and negative, that guide how we live out our lives.

These grow out of teachings we take on from social messaging, experiences, and what people have told us throughout our lives, and for some reason, it's easier to take on and listen to the negative.

To help in this, I've done a lot of work on my faith as well as practices that rewire my brain.

Through meditation, breathwork, study, dancing (where I feel most connected to God) and practicing my faith, I have truly come to know that God has made us all amazing and worthy. These practices have also helped ground me and connect me to my higher purpose.

Through Joe Dispenza's work, I have learned that when we change our thoughts, we change how our body responds through changes of the production of chemicals and hormones. When we change our bodies, we take different actions, which then create different realities.

I truly do not know where I would be if I didn't have my faith and my positive mindset actively working.

But to be frank, practicing these exercises doesn't mean that I have totally squashed the gremlins. I often have to tell them: "I know you're going to be here, but you can't be in the driver's seat; you've got to be in the passenger seat, and stay there. Thank you for being here. Thank you for trying to protect me. But I'm going to do this in a way that is much more empowering".

What does living a rich and prosperous life look like to you?

In the past, a rich and prosperous life looked like huge houses, swimming pools and nice cars...the epitome of the American dream.

This was the vision I had when growing up on food stamps and buying my clothes at garage sales.

Now, whilst I do love to be in beautiful and luxurious environments, I know now that the core of a rich and prosperous life looks like having amazing health, joy, healing, being around people who you love and lift you up, and self-actualization.

Also, a rich life has a sense of peace. So much of my life, I have lived in anxiety, fear, and feelings of "not enoughness", but these never allowed me to live the life that I'm supposed to live.

In the end, I was always chasing something outside of myself, but in reality, richness comes from within. When we get to the point of understanding this concept and then start creating from that place, that's where the riches are.

Through your feminine lens, what does it mean to be a leader?

To be a feminine leader is someone who understands the power of being female... the power of groundedness, graciousness, intuition, abundance, love, and wisdom. In answering this, I think of the archetypes, the warrior, the warrior princess, the magician, the Huntress, and the goddess.

When we tap into these elements as leaders, we can connect with people in so many ways. It's not forcing, it's allowing. It's standing tall and strong and speaking one's heart, while at the same time being able to be open to receive.

And, of course, there is also a need for the masculine side of things to be a leader, which is the doing, the structures, and the systems.

What role has vulnerability played in your success story?

Initially, in my branding, I thought I was to show something perfect, glossy, and glamorous, while not showing what I thought was the weak side or the side that would be easily judged. But what I found is that I was hiding. Hiding from my audience and ultimately from myself.

After trial and error, what I have found is that vulnerability allows us to be real with ourselves and others, which then attracts more people to us and our message. It allows us to connect with others because they see themselves in us and feel like they are not alone in this.

This journey toward allowing myself to be vulnerable has been a challenge, but incredibly empowering as well.

In doing so, I can just be me, and show all sides of me, which means I don't have to just show the glam with the lashes. I can show all the nuances of what makes me, me. And the more I do such, the more magnetic I am to clients who I can then impact, empower, and support to be more confident in themselves so that they too can make the impact that they need to make in the world.

Whether being interviewed or interviewing others, what role have these connected conversations played in your business?

Connected conversations through being interviewed or interviewing others have been incredibly powerful and important in my life and business because they offer new opportunities and experiences, otherwise not had.

They also help to expand my audience and touch and be touched by people who I might never have been in contact with before. It goes without saying that with an expansion of your network comes an expansion of more support, more new thoughts, and of course income.

What makes these types of conversations even more beautiful is that they have helped me reach people from all over the globe, many of whom are now in my community, have become clients and even friends.

What is the most difficult decision you have had to make to pursue your dreams?
The most difficult decision I've had to make to pursue my dreams (and one that I have re-make from time to time) has been the decision to BELIEVE that I am worthy of my dreams. Then the next challenge was to then act on that belief and follow through.

What are your core guiding values, and why?
Faith, integrity and creativity.

Faith has been the most difficult to follow because of my fluctuating lack of faith in myself. A while ago, I was speaking with my coach about the challenging time I was having, accepting that I could fulfill the huge visions we were creating, and I will never forget the question she asked me.

Do you have faith in God that this can happen?

It was like a bullet between the eyes.

It was in this moment, that even though in all my years of believing in God, I realised that I was trying to do it all myself rather than surrendering in faith.

If I was to be honest in myself, I really didn't have faith in Him.

This was definitely a wake-up call to live more in alignment and turn my faith to Him.

The second guiding value is integrity. One of my biggest fears is disappointing people. As a kid, if I disappointed my parents, it was like a gut punch to my solar plexus. Making them mad was one thing, but disappointing them hit to my core.

And this fear of disappointing people stuck throughout my life. So now I work toward having impeccable integrity instead of the fear of disappointing, taking action ensuring that there is nothing that makes me look back over my shoulder, wondering if I did something wrong.

My third guiding value is creativity, which is interwoven throughout my days because it inspires me and keeps me lit up. A sense of creativity and fun needs to be a part of everything that I do.

What top 3 things make you come alive?

Art of any kind makes me come alive. I literally can sit in front of a painting or a sculpture for hours and "watch" it because there's so much richness and so much movement in them.

The second thing that truly lights me up is dancing. Dancing, moving my body and expressing my experiences through movements is a drug for me.

There's nothing like it, nothing.

Last but not least, what also makes me come alive are the precious moments of pure love and joy, the snuggles, hugs, kisses and giggles with my family.

What self-love rituals do you prioritise and why?

I prioritise eating and sleeping well, and exercising.

I also love taking long hot baths with Epsom salts, essential oils and the soft glow of candlelight, as well as scheduled massages.

As an introvert, I also prioritize alone time to just be by myself, and it makes all the difference.

To make my self-care even more effective and powerful, I schedule it out on my calendar because otherwise, it likely will not happen. I know that for me to be the effective and present person I need to be for my family and business, I have to take care of myself in a joyful way.

Now that we are re-emerging after the pandemic, I am looking forward to scheduling a quarterly getaway, even if it's just one night. The change of scenery, and the quiet time, alone time can be profound for one's well being, health and mindset.

What is your favourite strategy to unhook from procrastination?

Action. Action. Action.

When you do just one action toward your goals, everything changes, and momentum begins again.

What would you say to the women who feel they should be able to do-it-all without a tribe/community/coach?

If you'd like to go faster, and do it with more joy, do it with a community and a coach.

I always have a coach who is one step ahead of me. No matter how far I am in my business, I can always find someone who is further along than I am, someone who will keep me on my toes, help me see my blind spots, challenge me to see bigger, believe bigger and hold me accountable for my actions.

In terms of a tribe and my group, I prioritize surrounding myself with people who lift me up, and who will allow me to lift them up. When you have a group of people you can trust, have fun with, be challenged by and love and be loved, you will never feel alone or lost.

Whose voice/s do you tune into for a guaranteed dose of inspiration?
Les Brown, Jen Gotleib, Brene Brown, and Lisa Bilyeu.

What role have coaches and/or masterminds played in your success?

Coaches and masterminds have played an integral part in my success because they have helped expand my mind and heart and provided countless opportunities in business and life.

Being a part of masterminds, especially, have blessed me with lifelong friendships across the globe who also connect me (and I, them) with people I might never have the opportunity to network with, which, in turn, have helped me create an international brand.

The members also always inspire and challenge me to be a better person with endless possibilities, which is priceless.

Do you think you would be where you are now without having worked with a coach and why or why not?
I know I would not be where I am without having worked with a coach. I would be so far behind where I am right now because I follow and allow those further ahead of me to guide me from their experiences, knowledge and expertise. Why recreate the wheel, and why not make my learning curve shorter than if I were to try and figure it all out on my own?

What are you most grateful for?

I am most grateful for this breath. And then next breath. And the next…because without my breath, I would not be able to experience all the other things I am grateful for.

What are your top 3 guilty pleasures?
Wine, chocolate, and going into expensive stores trying things on, feeling and believing I belong there and can shop there. The vibration is so high, and the quality of materials is often so exquisite to experience!

What qualities do you see when you say, "She is a PHENOMENAL WOMAN!"?

A phenomenal woman is always working toward self-actualization, so to be self-aware, more so than self-conscious.

She is guided by her principles.

She works toward excellence in all that she does, forgives herself and gives herself grace when she falters.

She allows herself to be vulnerable and shows her true sides. All her sides. Even the not so beautiful sides.

She leads from her heart.

She's creative and loves deeply.

She has a beautiful and powerful presence.

She makes other people feel beautiful, included, and powerful as she empowers them.

She brings beauty to the world.

She faces her challenges straight on, even when she's shaking in her boots and covered in dirt from falling.

She accomplishes great things and doesn't give up, even in the face of adversity.

She knows she's not perfect, but from the outside, she appears pretty amazing.

She laughs a lot and allows herself to cry freely when she feels the need.

She will always have open arms to hold others when they are crying as she knows the pain.

She knows why she came here at this time in history and understands her purpose. She courageously, boldly, and magnetically steps into the unknown out of her comfort zone through faith.

And finally, she shines her light brightly in the world, giving everyone else who she touches the opportunity to permit themselves to do the same.

Elizabeth de Moraes Links

instagram.com/iamelizabethdemoraes

facebook.com/ElizabethElideMoraes

tiktok.com/@elizabethdemoraes1111

www.elizabethdemoraes.com

Nellie Corriveau

FOUNDER AND HEAD COACH
AT THE SALES QUEEN.

Nellie Corriveau

Founder and Head Coach at The Sales Queen.

Ohio, United States

"... when I am in full joy and gratitude mode, the mean girls can't exist, and it is glorious!"

What has driven you to create the success that you have? (What is your WHY?)

I have so many answers to this question! My husband and daughter motivate me to be my best every day, and all the women I serve keep me going. More women get to make more money so that they can live the lives they really want to live. I know I was put on this planet to help show them the path.

If you were to choose 3 words that describe who you are as a woman, what would they be?

Courageous, creative and kind!

What role has vision boards and/or clearly defined goals played in your life and business?

A huge role! I have multiple vision boards in multiple locations, so they are always front and centre and remind me why I am putting in the hard work!

How do you quieten the shame gremlins that say 'who do you think you are' or 'you're not enough'?

This is a daily choice! I have noticed when I am too busy serving and supporting others; my mean girls don't have an opportunity to speak up. Also, when I am in full joy and gratitude mode, the mean girls can't exist, and it is glorious!

What does living a rich and prosperous life look like to you?

It looks like living and giving without looking at my bank account! Being able to do anything we want, go anywhere we desire and support others along the way too!

Through your feminine lens, what does it mean to be a leader?

A leader wants to help others shine as much as she possibly can. She is also okay with being different and speaking up for herself, inspiring others to do the same.

What role has vulnerability played in your success story?

I have noticed my audience LOVES when I open up, speak my mind, show up with no makeup, and just be me. They say it is refreshing! The more I do it, the more pressure it takes off me to be perfect. I want to show you can build a business, live your life, and have fun doing it with a family, even when you have setbacks! I share a ton with my audience, and I never want to stop that.

Whether being interviewed or interviewing others, what role have these connected conversations played in your business?

They are everything to me!!!!!! I have met some dear friends through interviews, and some have become clients and colleagues. My life would be drastically different without meeting them.

What is the most difficult decision you have had to make to pursue your dreams?

To step down from my leadership position at the nonprofit organization I created. I built it for ten years, and when I had a family, it was time to pass the torch to the next leader. It was such a hard decision to make, but I knew I needed to in order to make my dreams come true.

What are your core guiding values, and why?

I have so many, but the one I live by every day is to treat others the way you would want to be treated. I strive to be kind every day in big and small ways. I know this world needs more of it too.

What makes you come alive?

I light up when I hear women making more money! Even if it's a small sale because I know what that does for their confidence!

What self-love rituals do you prioritise and why?

So many! Working out, good sleep, journaling, and water are some things that I know help me be my best self!

What is your favourite strategy to unhook from procrastination?

I need deadlines!!!! I also ask for help from my team and husband to keep me focused and on track. I love a good list to brain dump all the tasks too!

What would you say to the women who feel they should be able to do-it-all without a tribe/community/coach?

Don't do it! You deserve all the love and support around you every step of the way!

Whose voices do you tune into for a guaranteed dose of inspiration?

It depends on the day! Tony Robbins always helps get me inspired or chatting with my clients and hearing their hopes and dreams!

What role have coaches and/or masterminds played in your success?

I can tell when I have a coach and enrolled in masterminds and when I am not. I play a much bigger game when I have that high level of accountability around me.

Do you think you would be where you are now without having worked with a coach and why or why not?

No! I would be very lonely, confused and also not having as much fun. It's worth every penny!

What are you most grateful for?

I am most grateful for my clients and family. I feel so blessed to have them and to be able to support them. Every day I wake up is another day to play a bigger game and support others.

What are your guilty pleasures?

Oh, I have so many! I love a good meal from a fancy restaurant, binging a Netflix show, putting together outfits, planning trips and crazy enough working out!

What qualities do you see when you say, "She is a PHENOMENAL WOMAN!"?

She is unstoppable! She is beautiful and owns it! She wants to support other women! She embraces her flaws and failures. She loves to learn. She wants to make the world a better place! She is loving. She is daring and loves life to the fullest!

Nellie Corriveau Links

instagram.com/ the_sales_queen

facebook.com/SalesQueenCoaching

tiktok.com/@the_sales_queen

www.salesqueencoaching.com

Rebecca Whitman

AUTHOR, COACH, FOUNDER OF
ELEGANT WARRIOR TRAINING.

PHENOMENAL FEMININE ENTREPRENEURS

Rebecca Whitman

Author, Coach, Founder of Elegant Warrior Training.

California, United States

"So to me, the most successful person in the room is the happiest person in the room."

What has driven you to create the success that you have? (What is your WHY?)

I want to create a Legacy. I want people to have felt my presence, my love and my service. And I want people to remember me in a positive way and what I stood for. I don't want to have any regrets. I want to just use up every second every moment of my life to get the most out of it.

If you were to choose 3 words that describe who you are as a woman, what would they be?

Bold, intelligent, and funny.

What role has vision boards and/or clearly defined goals played in your life and business?

I have been doing vision boards since I was a kid since before they were called vision boards. We used to call them collages. And we would cut out images of what we aspired to, and create collages. We even put images in our locker. In fact, in one of the classes I teach, we write out our goals for every area of life. I call these key aspects of life the Seven Pillars of Abundance. I like to say that a goal is a dream with a plan.

How do you quieten the shame gremlins that say 'who do you think you are' or 'you're not enough'?

I combat negative self talk with affirmations. For example, I have three affirmations that I say when I hear myself say, "I'm not enough."

"I am enough. I have enough. I am willing to set myself free." I am willing, because we are the ones that create our own prisons with our negative narrative.

Another affirmation that I really like, is "I'm exactly where I'm supposed to be,", because one of my Gremlins is perfectionism.

If I take the words "would have," "could have," and "should have" out of my inner dialogue, then there are not many words left to beat myself up.

What does living a rich and prosperous life look like to you?

Happiness is success. Most people define rich and prosperous by how much money you have. But in my opinion, you can have all the money in the world, but if you're miserable, then what's the point? So to me, the most successful person in the room is the happiest person in the room.

So when I go to a high school or college reunion, I'm not looking to see who made the most money or has the most social status; I'm looking to see who's the most joyful.

So I want to be the happiest person in the room and happy in my life because that's the whole point of coming here to planet earth is to experience joy.

Through your feminine lens, what does it mean to be a leader?

The masculine paradigm of leadership is pushing people to be better, whereas the feminine paradigm of leadership is inspiring people, motivating people to find the strength, the goals and the fortitude within themselves.

To me, all great leaders, male and female, lead by example. Nobody wants to follow a personal trainer who's 50 pounds overweight and chain smoking. People want to be inspired by their personal trainer because their personal trainer is in shape. And leadership is the same way. My mission is to lead women to be unapologetically authentic, so that they can live their life with resilience, grit and grace. Therefore, I get to be unapologetically authentic.

And if I am leading by example, I am going to find my tribe who also aspires to be unapologetically authentic.

What role has vulnerability played in your success story?

Vulnerability is not something that came naturally to me. I grew up as a competitive tennis player, by the age of eight, I was playing in national tournaments. I was taught to be really tough and to win. Being vulnerable is something that I have learned as an adult. I really want to connect with my audience. I know that if everything looks perfect on my feed, then I'm not going to have real connections with people. In other words, if I really want to connect with people, they get to see the good, the bad and the ugly.

Everyday I am learning to be more real, more authentic, more vulnerable. Messy is totally okay. Vulnerability is a quality I admire in others and will continue to cultivate in myself.

Whether being interviewed or interviewing others, what role have these connected conversations played in your business?

Having a connected conversation with someone is magical. It makes me feel alive. It makes me feel like I'm in my heart. It makes me feel vulnerable. Having a connected conversation is really experiencing someone's humanity and connecting with their soul. In the workspace, people will do business with you if they like, know and trust you.

When you're having connected conversations with your clients, you learn what they want, what their vision is and what their pain points are.

Having a connected conversation means you are really listening. Listening is a lost art form. We have two ears and one mouth because we're supposed to listen twice as much as we speak.

What is the most difficult decision you have had to make to pursue your dreams?

My decision to get divorced after three years of marriage was my most difficult decision. I was 39 when I met my ex-husband. I thought, "Oh, my God, this is the last house on the block. If I don't have a baby with this man, then I will miss the opportunity to be a mother." I ended up putting a lot of pressure on him to become my dream guy. But, of course, he resented me for not accepting him as he was. And I was constantly upset because he was not fulfilling my expectations of what a husband should do. I am grateful that I didn't have a child with him because that would have been really challenging.

I got to learn the lesson that it's more important to feel good than to look good. We looked so happy and in love on our social media, but we really weren't. To step into my next greatest version of myself, I had to be willing to walk away from a relationship that wasn't serving me. I had to be willing to look bad; I had to be willing to fail. Now, four years later, I am engaged to the love of my life, and he is everything that I want in a man. There's no biological clock ticking, and we've known each other already for over three years. This marriage is fueled by love, and the other marriage was driven by

What are your core guiding values, and why?

My first value is fun. If it's not fun, what's the point? We're not here just to work and toil. So my whole philosophy in life is I don't live to work; I work to live. I own four businesses. I am a self-made millionaire through my assets. But I am not obsessed with money. I am obsessed with living a 360-degree lifestyle, where I have all Seven Pillars of abundance in balance. I have a great spirituality. I have a wonderful fitness regimen. I'm wildly in love with my fiance. I have time to walk my dog twice a day. I have time to meet a friend for coffee and catch up.

My second core value is freedom. If you're working a job, you get an hourly wage or yearly salary. And in both instances, you're trading time for money. Time is finite and limited. If you're trading time for money, there are only 40 hours in a workweek or 52 weeks in a year. I want financial freedom. I've been in commission sales for over 25 years. And I love it. Because I get paid what I'm worth, I don't get paid for my time. Having money gives you freedom. I don't want money for money's sake, but I want money for freedom's sake. Money gives you the freedom to do what you want, when you want, where you want, and with who you want. That is true freedom. Money is the energy that generates freedom in your life, and that is worth striving for.

My third core value is vitality. Health and wellness are so important to me that one of my income streams is a health and wellness company. I was an aerobics instructor in high school. I've always taken supplements. I've always really wanted to take care of my body because health is wealth. If you have your health, you have everything. You can create anything, from the point of being a healthy person. If you don't have your health, you can still be financially successful. But if you're stuck at home in bed and can't go out and enjoy life, then what is the point?

What are the top 3 things that make you come alive?

1. Music, 2. My dog, 3. Exercise

What self-love rituals do you prioritise and why?

Self-love is so so so important to me. When a woman practices self-love, she pours from a full cup. As women, we are trained to give and neglect our own self-care. The number one thing for me is to sleep seven to eight hours a night.

The other thing that I do is a morning practice. I have an amazing life-changing journal format, which I have been doing since I was 19. I actually have so many God journals that I could pile them from the floor to the ceiling. They have changed my life because they changed my thinking from negative to positive. I met the woman who gave me the journal format when I was 19. And she was never to be seen again. I really think she was an angel. I try to do the journal in the morning; if I don't do it in the morning, I do it at night.

Another self-love ritual is yoga and meditation. I try to do meditation every day; I don't do it perfectly, there are some days that I miss. I really love the Insight Timer app because I can find a meditation that fits into the increment of time I have available. Sometimes it feels good just to be still, breathe and listen to get out of my head.

What is your favourite strategy to unhook from procrastination?

Procrastination is such an enemy. Because it's so much easier to say, "I'll do it later." But when I take action, the second it comes up, it won't end up on my list of things to do. If I write it on my Things To Do list, it might happen in a week or two. If I take care of it in the moment, then it's done. And it's off my list. Like that old Nike ad says, "just do it."

If somebody's name pops into my head, that's my divine guidance. If I forget to write their name down or forget to call them, I might not ever get that download again. But if I act on it right away, I make the call, and it's done. So the best way to get unhooked from procrastination is to take action right away.

What would you say to the women who feel they should be able to do-it-all without a tribe/community/coach?

I would say you can, but it's not going to be as fun, it's not going to be as smooth, it's a much harder road.

I am an advocate of the success principle: find somebody who has what you want. And if you do what they did, you can get what they got. Whatever industry you're in, you find someone in that industry who's a mentor or a coach. If they're willing to show you how to do it, follow their lead. If somebody has the tools that you need to make your journey easier. Why wouldn't you take it? I know a lot of women are scared to invest in themselves. But you're investing in yourself, your goals, your dreams and your vision.

There's no better investment than yourself. And if you stay on that path, you will eventually make your money back. I wouldn't have the romantic relationship, the business or the podcast that I have without hiring coaches to help me and support me. Having a community that is cheering you on, guiding you and inspiring you makes all the difference in the world. I like to say that community creates immunity. Find your tribe.

Whose voice/s do you tune into for a guaranteed dose of inspiration?

A business mentor Jessie Lee Ward inspires me with her unapologetic authenticity. She is the number one money earner female in network marketing, and she has an incredible podcast called "The People's Mentor."

The other voice I tune into for inspiration is Abraham Hicks. I like their YouTube videos. If I'm feeling down, I'm not in the same space after the video. Their message helps me stay calm and put things in perspective.

What role have coaches and/or masterminds played in your success?

I really like the mastermind concept because I get to learn from everybody's questions and input. God speaks through other people.

Do you think you would be where you are now without having worked with a coach and why or why not?

I would not be where I am without coaching. I would not have the "Balanced, Beautiful, Abundant" show, which was ranked top 5% globally in the world for podcasts.

My romantic relationship style is something I learned about through coaching. Everything I have accomplished financially in my sales career and my network marketing business is from coaches. I have an incredible coach, Sarah Zolecki, who is the top female money earner in a health and wellness company. I joined this company for the opportunity to be coached by Sarah, who is making seven figures and willing to take me under her wing. Thanks to her, this venture has been quite lucrative!

What are you most grateful for?

I am the most grateful just to be alive. So being alive. Having the chance to be on planet Earth, eating the food, smell the smells, hug the people, learn the lessons, make the connections, be in love, and go for my dreams.

What are your top 3 guilty pleasures?

1. Celebrity Gossip
2. Caffeine
3. Online Shopping

What qualities do you see when you say, "She is a PHENOMENAL WOMAN!"?

I see a woman who is in her power. I see an authentic woman who feels comfortable in her body, whatever body size she has. I see a woman who is strong and who makes empowered choices. I see a woman who is not a people pleaser, doesn't care about what people think and knows how to please herself. I see a woman who knows how to connect and have successful relationships, not just in business but also romantically and socially. I see a woman who feels beautiful. I see a woman who has positive energy and a positive mindset. You can feel her positive energy when she walks into the room.

Rebecca Whitman Links

instagram.com/rebeccaewhitman

www.rebeccaelizabethwhitman.com

facebook.com/rebecca.whitman

twitter.com/rebeccaewhitman

Top 5% ranked podcast globally is

www.balancedbeautifulabundant.buzzsprout.com

Ana Paula Nunoz

PEAK PERFORMANCE COACH & INTUITIVE,
CO-FOUNDER @INAURA_OFFICIAL.

Ana Paula Munoz

Peak Performance Coach & Intuitive,
Co-Founder @inaura_official.

California, United States

*"It is key in my life because the moment
I started being vulnerable. I started
being REAL.. my true me"*

**If you were to choose words that describe who you are as
a woman, what would they be?**
1. Aware
2. Unapologetic #anapaulagetic
3. Sensual
4. Creatrix: Creating through Feminine

**What role have vision boards and/or clearly defined goals played
in your life and business?**
Vision is PRIMARY in my life, relationships, business. It is the filter
through which all passes through.

I've had a vision board for years.

**How do you quieten the shame gremlins that say 'who do you
think you are' or 'you're not enough'?**
I exist in possibility most of the time. My mind, body, spirit practices
are key for maintaining an expansive and aware way of being...
It is key for my alignment. When I align with my essence and vision,
these 'gremlins' don't show up.

When and if they do... I befriend them, acknowledge them and get
to know them intimately. I treat them as fragmented parts of me that
I now have the opportunity to know.

What does living a rich and prosperous life look like to you?

Abundant mindset, creating with flow, remaining in my sensuality; being magnetic to my desires.

Through your feminine lens, what does it mean to be a leader?

It means to lead with heart, magnetism, vibrance. Embrace the creative chaos of the feminine with the support of the structured discerning masculine.

What role has vulnerability played in your success story?

It is key in my life because the moment I started being vulnerable. I started being REAL.. my true me.

It has allowed for honesty, full expression, and for my unique essence to shine through.

Whether being interviewed or interviewing others, what role have these connected conversations played in your business?

I love both of these! They haven't played a huge role... I feel so fired up after!

What is the most difficult decision you have had to make to pursue your dreams?

Leave my corporate career "dream job", let go of my families beliefs of what success should look like, leap into the unknown when I wasn't friends with it yet.

What are your core guiding values, and why?

1. Stay true to your Essence.
2. Feel into Your Heart.
3. You are Endless Possibility.

What top 3 things make you come alive?

I love the depth that we reach in healing and transformation work! When my clients can understand and transform a belief that has lived within them their whole life. When they can integrate and befriend a part of them they were previously scared to acknowledge. When we create a beautiful closure to a trauma that had been with them for years. It breaks open my heart to witness and be a support and guide in these transformations!

What self-love rituals do you prioritise and why?

1. Delight in sensuality.
2. Be kind to all the parts of me.
3. Speak kindly to myself.

What is your favourite strategy to unhook from procrastination?

Start with one small thing.

What would you say to the women who feel they should be able to do-it-all without a tribe/community/coach?

Ou, yes! I know this one well. I've been there, sister! I would say: Sister; you CAN do it alone, but at the cost of WHAT?

What if you could have it all and create it all through a different pathway. Fully integrating your feminine and creating a structure that works FOR you vs. staying plugged into the way of creating you grew up with.

What role have coaches and/or masterminds played in your success?

A huge role for taking me to the next level and showing me things I hadn't seen before. I continue to go deeper and deeper, and it's a lifetime commitment to keep going. The deeper I go in me, the deeper I can support my clients!

Do you think you would be where you are now without having worked with a coach and why or why not?

No way.

What are you most grateful for?

The level of relating I enjoy every day because of this work. That is true freedom for me... to be able to connect SO deeply with my partner, my clients, my community.

What are your top 3 guilty pleasures?

1. Definitely Lily's Salted Caramel Chocolate
2. Hazelnut Hu Chocolate
3. Organic Apples with Almond Butter

What qualities do you see when you say, "She is a PHENOMENAL WOMAN!"?

An embodied woman who is spiritually aware deeply connected to her essence, vision, and heart.

Ana Paula Munoz Links

🔲 *instagram.com/iamanapaulamunoz*

🔲 *instagram.com/inaura_official*

🔲 *facebook.com/tiamanapaulamunoz*

🌐 *www.anapaulamunoz.com*

🌐 *www.inaura.com*

Krista Mashore

BEST SELLING AUTHOR & FOUNDER
OF KRISTA MASHORE COACHING.

Krista Mashore

Best Selling Author & Founder of
Krista Mashore Coaching.

California, United States

"I really believe in the power of mindset and that your thoughts become things. What you think about becomes your actions, which then becomes your life."

What has driven you to create the success that you have? (What is your WHY?)

My 'why' was my daughters. After going through an unexpected divorce, I chose to jump into Real Estate full-time so I could take care of my girls. They were definitely my 'why' in the beginning. Now that I coach agents from across the country and teach them how to have more financial freedom and time my why is that I'm able to serve and help people so that we can all have the best kind of life possible.

If you were to choose 3 words that describe who you are as a woman, what would they be?

Positive, Motivating and Contributor

What role has vision boards and/or clearly defined goals played in your life and business?

Oh my gosh, this is a good one. I love vision boards. Three years ago, I put a two comma club award on my vision board, an award that shows I generated over a million dollars in online sales. I have another big one that shows that we did over $10 million online. I got this one after I put it on my vision board, wrote my name on it and took a picture of it. And about a year later, we had one, and we've gotten several since then.

I write out my goals for the day, my goals for the year, envision my life as I want it to be in the future, and have used vision boards to keep me focused. I have pictures on my vision board of me starting a coaching program and helping people, which have all come true. I absolutely believe in the power of visualization and in being the creator of your own destiny.

How do you quieten the shame gremlins that say 'who do you think you are' or 'you're not enough'?

This is definitely something that I've had to struggle with. I am somebody who hasn't lived at home since I was 13. I found myself in a group home then in a foster home, after running away from home. So I have absolutely had to battle with feeling like I'm not worthy enough, or I'm not good enough, or that people won't like me. And I've just made it a constant work in progress. In fact, I'm still working on it. I read books like crazy.

Whenever I'm finding myself being negative, which isn't very often, I'll wear a bracelet that I snap anytime I think a negative thought or go to make a negative comment. I really believe in the power of mindset and that your thoughts become things. What you think about becomes your actions, which then becomes your life.

For this reason, I'm mindful of what I say to myself. I've had to overcome imposter syndrome and learn to feel worthy. I've worked on it so, so much and so, so hard that now... I finally actually believe it.

What does living a rich and prosperous life look like to you?

It's having a balance of health, wealth, relationships, and contribution. If you're not healthy, you can't be wealthy, right? And if you're not healthy, you can't have a good relationship.

Living in abundance in all aspects of life is not just about money; it's about being a good person and treating others with respect and kindness.

And I think that you can get that from having great rituals, routines and habits. Also, surrounding yourself with like-minded people and people who inspire you.

Through your feminine lens, what does it mean to be a leader?

To be a leader means to inspire and help others and encourage others to want to take action and change their lives. I've made it a personal goal over the past year and a half to be a better leader within my own company and to make sure my team members really enjoy working for me.

At times in the past, I've been hard on people and really expected more than I should have. I didn't convey the messaging to them in the right way, so I've been working on just trying to be the very best leader that I can be in my own company. I believe in eating my own dog food; anything that I preach, I practice, so I don't teach things I don't do.

What role has vulnerability played in your success story?

When I went through my divorce and told people about it, people were inspired by it. I've also dealt with some personal abuse and trauma, and I've just recently started talking about that. It has amazed me just how receptive people have been. I think people often make assumptions about others and about why they're successful or who they are.

They tell themselves these lies about, "Oh, that person's just has it easier," or, "They must just be naturally that way," or "They must have been born successful," or whatever it might be. And I think by telling my story about where I've come from, it's really helped people understand that anybody can achieve anything if they put their mind to it.

Whether being interviewed or interviewing others, what role have these connected conversations played in your business?

Oh, wow. Proximity is key. I will tell you that it's opened up so many different doors for me, being around inspiring people. It's helped me to be able to get to know people; it's helped people get to know me, it's led to some amazing relationships, it's led to me being able to be on some massive stages to able to make a bigger impact. So I think it's very important.

What are your core guiding values, and why?

Being abundant in all aspects of life. I love to contribute. I believe contribution equals growth. I take my family very seriously and my marriage very seriously. I love being a leader and treating people with respect, and inspiring and encouraging others.

What top 3 things make you come alive?

Honestly, it is just helping people. I love people. I always say people before things and things will come. So as long as you're getting encouraged and inspiring others, you'll grow. The more you give, the more you get. That's not why I give, but it always comes back by giving to other people.

What self-love rituals do you prioritise and why?

Hydrating! I wake up every morning and drink a quarter gallon of water before I even leave my bedroom; then, I drink another quarter gallon when I go to the gym. I try to go to the gym five days a week.

Writing down what I'm grateful for every day. Then I write out my six to-do's for the day and then visualize the success that I'm going to have. Then, at the end of the day, I celebrate my successes. Focusing on what I'm doing right, not what I'm doing wrong, because you get what you think about. And, of course, I love taking care of my family.

What is your favourite strategy to unhook from procrastination?

Just do it. I mean, honestly, just do it. Do the things you don't like first and get them done because you'll have more energy, and success breeds success. Because you're getting it done first-up and succeeding, that momentum continues throughout the day.

Whose voice/s do you tune into for a guaranteed dose of inspiration?

Tony Robbins. Mel Robbins. Dean Graziosi. Russell Brunson.

What role have coaches and/or masterminds played in your success?

Absolutely everything. I will tell you that I have spent hundreds of thousands of dollars on coaching, and that's not an exaggeration. I would not be where I am today if it wasn't for hiring Russell Brunson and joining his Inner circle. It's absolutely paid off. You need to pay, to pay attention if that makes sense. Also, who you surround yourself with is everything. And those relationships have paid off tenfold.

Do you think you would be where you are now without having worked with a coach and why or why not?

Absolutely not. Because when you hire a coach, you're able to learn from their mistakes. You're able to gain from their successes. You're able to fast track your success, and they're able to help push you and give you ideas that you wouldn't have thought of on your own. I've had a communications coach. I have digital marketing coaches. I have social media coaches. I've had business coaches. I have had pretty much every kind of coach you can imagine.

What are you most grateful for?

I am grateful for where I'm at in life right now. I'm so grateful for my team. I'm grateful for the relationship that I have with my husband and for his loving spirit. I'm grateful for my daughters. I'm grateful for the fact that I have a happy, upbeat attitude.

I'm grateful for the life that I've created. I'm grateful for my beginnings because my beginnings got me where I am today. I'm grateful for the relationship that I have with my parents now. I'm grateful for my extended family. I'm grateful for the business that I have. I love what I do. I'm passionate about it. I love being able to help people. I'm so grateful for all of that.

What are your top 3 guilty pleasures?

I love cooking, and I love food. That's one of my guilty pleasures for sure. I do love wine as well. And I love going out on our boat.

What qualities do you see when you say, "She is a PHENOMENAL WOMAN!"?

I think of somebody who is very giving and kind. A true leader who helps others and inspires other women. She wants to pull people up, not push people down and is confident in her own skin. Confident enough to be real. I love real women that don't try to be someone that they're not.

Krista Mashore Links

[instagram icon] *instagram.com/kristamashore*

[facebook icon] *facebook.com/krista.vitalemashore*

[globe icon] *www.kristamashore.com*

I think of somebody who is very giving and kind. A true leader who helps others and inspires other women. She wants to pull people up, not push people down and is confident in her own skin. Confident enough to be real. I love real women that don't try to be someone that they're not.

KRISTA MASHORE

Christa Nichols

SALES CONVERSION COPYWRITER AND
MESSAGING EXPERT. FOUNDER OF WRITTEN
RESULTS ACADEMY AND THE THE COPY FIX.

Christa Nichols

Sales conversion copywriter and messaging expert. Founder of Written Results Academy and The Copy Fix.

Iowa, United States

"It felt super vulnerable to take the initial leap into entrepreneurship. I wasn't equipped to run a business. I was scared it wouldn't succeed and worried that I wasn't enough - but I did it anyway."

What has driven you to create the success that you have? (What is your WHY?)

I want other women to know what is possible for them too. That they can create a business that's their own, that's not dependent on a boss or a paycheck. That they can create a business they love. And that they can work with clients who treat them well from all over the world.

As a farm wife and mom from Iowa who started with just a little bit of raw talent and the desire to learn whatever I didn't know. I am now committed to mentoring and training copywriters, so together, we can raise the standards for copywriters everywhere while providing copywriters with the skills training needed to get results for their clients.

If I can do it, you can do it too!

If you were to choose 3 words that describe who you are as a woman, what would they be?

Connective, Intuitive, Loyal.

What role has vision boards and/or clearly defined goals played in your life and business?

I never used to dream big dreams or have goals. I had this strange idea that if I dreamed it and it didn't come true, I'd just be letting myself and everyone else down. I didn't want to seem ungrateful, so I focused on being content with what I had.

That worked great until "what I had" wasn't a viable option anymore. I realized that my whole adult life, I'd been playing it safe. I wasn't content, I was complacent, and that had to change.

I never knew I was capable of running a business or achieving the things I've achieved in such a short period of time.

But once I got that first taste of possibility, I was hooked and found myself asking, "What else could I do if I tried? What else am I capable of?"

I joined a professional mastermind, and that was my first exposure to setting a vision and goals for my business. It was so scary at first, but I did it and learned to celebrate not just the successes but the learning along the way.

I'll always invest in masterminds. I have found that I love the accountability and motivation masterminds provide.

How do you quieten the shame gremlins that say 'who do you think you are' or 'you're not enough'?

I remind myself that the more I accomplish, the more people I can impact and serve. I don't do what I do just for me, and playing small or giving in to imposter syndrome won't help anyone. Being able to serve at a higher level is a huge motivator for me.

What does living a rich and prosperous life look like to you?

It doesn't look like a number to me. It looks more like freedom. We're blessed with the freedom to live the kind of life we want to live without worrying about finances, the freedom to work when and how we want, and the freedom to create. We get to give more of our time and resources to our community and those in need. And we can show our two teenagers that doing things the traditional way of college then a career working for someone else isn't the only path.

Through your feminine lens, what does it mean to be a leader?

I think it means being willing to step up and do the hard things, show up for your business every day, and be accountable and accept responsibility for the successes and failures that come.

It means seeking to better yourself so you can be a good boss for your team members, making wise choices about your personal life and how you divide your time and taking care of yourself because if you don't take care of yourself, you can't take care of anyone else.

What role has vulnerability played in your success story?

Everyone has a story, and it's a gift to be able to share it because you never know who it will encourage. I'm happy to be able to say that I started from nothing. I don't mind sharing the rough times, sleepless nights, epic failures, high stress, and nightmare client stories because it's all part of the journey to where I am today.

It felt super vulnerable to take the initial leap into entrepreneurship. I wasn't equipped to run a business. I was scared it wouldn't succeed and worried that I wasn't enough - but I did it anyway.

Feeling vulnerable isn't a sign you shouldn't take the leap. It's just a sign that you're human.

Whether being interviewed or interviewing others, what role have these connected conversations played in your business?

I love podcasts and interviews. I often get asked to speak in summits as well, and I've found that they're a great tool for growing your following because you are getting in front of another person's engaged audience. Their viewers know, like, and trust them, and now they'll know, like, and trust you too.

What is the most difficult decision you have had to make to pursue your dreams?

When I first started in digital marketing, I had a position as an ads strategist inside a Facebook ads agency. It was there that I learned everything I know about paid traffic, and it was there that I first started writing for sales. I was pretty good at it, and soon I was taking on sales copywriting projects on the side.

I loved that agency - still do. It was a balm for my soul and a safe place to regain my confidence after losing my first business. But there came a time when I had to make a choice. My private sales copywriting services were becoming more and more in demand. I wasn't going to be able to keep up with all the ads clients and copywriting projects.

I was going to have to choose. Should I stay in the agency, my safe space with guaranteed income and lots of support?

Or should I take a chance on having my own business again and go out on my own as a sales copywriter? I put off the decision for as long as I could, then finally, with my husband's support (or rather, push and shove), I gave my notice with the agency and started Christa Nichols Copy.

We tripled our monthly income within 30 days and never looked back. It was a hard choice, but it was the right one.

What are your core guiding values, and why?

I highly value family and community. There's no way I'd be where I am today without the support and encouragement of my tribe, some of which are related by blood and others by shared experience and entrepreneurial spirit.

I also value integrity. I strive always to do what I say and say what I do. Things should look the same outside m y business as they are on the inside.

I'm extremely loyal, and I work hard to maintain healthy, strong relationships.

Finally, I am committed to uncovering truth and nurturing faith. These core values help equip me to show up every day and make the world a better place.

What makes you come alive?

I love to spend time with family and friends doing anything that makes me laugh. Laughing is my favorite. I'm also a huge fan of travelling to new places and getting out of my everyday environment.

I'm pretty competitive, so any time I feel like I've had a big win for a client or in my own programs, I can't help but celebrate it.

What self-love rituals do you prioritise and why?

My husband and I like to get couples massages together. We probably do that once a month. Other than that, I'm really not very good at practising self-care. It's hard for me to slow down long enough.

What is your favourite strategy to unhook from procrastination?

I force myself to record how I spend my working hours. This helps a ton because I don't want to write down that I spent an hour watching TikTok videos and eating Cheetos.

I'll also go outside and take a walk to clear my head. Works wonders.

And sometimes, if I'm on a deadline and it's just not flowing, I'll leave my phone in the other room, shut myself in the office, and tell myself to just focus on the project for 30 minutes. If it's still not flowing, I can try something else. More often than not, by the time 30 minutes is up, I'm totally in flow again and making progress.

What would you say to the women who feel they should be able to do-it-all without a tribe/community/coach?

Sis, don't. Don't do that to yourself. Needing a tribe or community isn't an indication of weakness. It's actually an indication of strength because it shows you're willing to put aside your pride and ask for help if you need it. Plus everything is more fun with friends!

Whose voices do you tune into for a guaranteed dose of inspiration?

I love Brene Brown, Myron Golden, Francis Chan, Eugene Cho, Jen Hatmaker, and my husband and mom.

What role have coaches and/or masterminds played in your success?

I hired my first coach within months of starting digital marketing, even though it didn't make sense financially at the time, and it made all the difference.

I have absolute certainty that coaching and masterminds are valuable, and I will always invest in getting the support I need for my business.

Being part of coaching programs and masterminds has put me in the right places at the right times in terms of networking. It's given me access to encouragement and support when I needed it. And it's helped me grow my skill sets and make friendships that will last a lifetime.

Do you think you would be where you are now without having worked with a coach and why or why not?

100% the answer to that is no. I definitely would NOT be. The first coach I ever had believed in me when I didn't believe in myself. That alone was worth so much. My coaches have also shown me what's possible to achieve because they've achieved it before me. And my coaches have become my friends, too. They've introduced me to others who have inspired (and hired!) me.

What are you most grateful for?

My family. My husband and I have two healthy kids who are just plain good people that we're so proud of. And speaking of husband, he's my rock. He has been my number one fan and an amazing support system through this entrepreneurial journey.

He has stepped in to help in so many ways and still thinks I'm pretty even after more than 20 years of marriage. I'm blessed.

I'm also grateful for the freedom to grow a business and the ability to decide what kind of life we want to live and pursue it.

What are your guilty pleasures?

Reading fiction and eating cookies. Preferably together, but they're okay on their own, too.

What qualities do you see when you say, "She is a PHENOMENAL WOMAN!"?

Selflessness, perseverance, wisdom, generosity, and strength.

Christa Nichols Links

[instagram icon] instagram.com/christanicholscopy

[facebook icon] facebook.com/christanicholscopy

[youtube icon] youtube.com/christanicholscopy

[tiktok icon] tiktok.com/@christanicholscopy

[web icon] www.christanichols.com

Christine Innes

FOUNDER OF THE CORPORATE ESCAPISTS
MAGAZINE | PODCAST | TV SHOW #1
INTERNATIONAL BEST-SELLING AUTHOR.

Christine Innes

Founder of The Corporate Escapists
Magazine | Podcast | TV Show #1
International Best-Selling Author.

Queensland, Australia

*"Dreaming allows you to escape, but to follow
your dreams you need to know who you are.
To take full ownership of you - flaws and all."*

**What has driven you to create the success that you have?
(What is your WHY?)**

My driver has been to take control of my own life. For so long,
it had been driven by external influences. Stepping back into the
driver's seat again and resetting my own internal GPS.

**If you were to choose 3 words that describe who you are as
a woman, what would they be?**

Authentic, kind and passionate.

**What role has vision boards and/or clearly defined goals played
in your life and business?**

They have been key. I have a goal for my life, I use my own "create
your ideal life" worksheets to get clear on my goals. This then allows
me to clearly visualize what I want to create in my life and business.
The vision board also needs to be fluid as we grow and our goals
change.

**How do you quieten the shame gremlins that say 'who do you
think you are' or 'you're not enough'?**

I love these questions. The way I have learnt is to give the inner
critic a name.

You know the inner voice inside of you that constantly tells you that
you are not enough. Giving them a name allows me to tell them to
go away and that I don't need to listen to them.

It is also important to know what is no longer serving you as a person
and what is good for you.

The inner critic will want you to play small to stop your own shining light. So when you want to shine, and they stop you, tell them to leave.

What does living a rich and prosperous life look like to you?
It is filled with love. Love for the people around me and love for the things that are important in my life.

Money doesn't define a good life; it is the love for yourself and others that will give you the most reward. When we love who we are, we can allow more goodness into our lives. It all starts with the US.

Through your feminine lens, what does it mean to be a leader?
Being authentic. Knowing who you are and being able to stand in your own power. To allow your femininity to shine through, to allow all of your goodness to shine. We also need to accept all of us. As human beings, we are perfectly imperfect and it is essential that we accept that we make mistakes. This is how we grow as a leader and show others how to be the best version of themself.

What role has vulnerability played in your success story?
It has been key. Knowing myself and being able to show when I have made mistakes and taking ownership of them. This is being vulnerable. This is showing up as your true authentic self.

Being vulnerable allows you to accept yourself and others as they are,

As human beings, we are perfectly imperfect, and we need to allow ourselves to make mistakes and learn from the good and not so good.

Whether being interviewed or interviewing others, what role have these connected conversations played in your business?

I love stories. Stories helped me change my life, and now I have the opportunity to share other peoples stories. We often underestimate the power of stories and how they can connect, empower and inspire people.

By using stories, I have changed my life. I went from being broke, broken, in a toxic and unfixable marriage to now living the life of my dreams.

I get to inspire others with my own personal story now, which is all from creating connections.

We need to understand the importance of connections personally and professionally for everyone to take ownership of their own story and allow them to dream their own ending.

What is the most difficult decision you have had to make to pursue your dreams?

Finding out who I was. Dreaming allows you to escape, but you need to know who you are to follow your dreams. To take full ownership of you - flaws and all.

When I did this and found my core values, wrote my own mission and vision statement, it completely changed my direction in my life as I was back in control and had a firm foundation to stand on.

What are your core guiding values, and why? It is Authenticity, love and trust.

Authenticity - to always show up as me. To accept my flaws and learn from all the lessons in my life. Without this, I am still masking who I am. Not showing up and owning my life. NO more suit of armour to hide me from the world.

Love - love for myself and love for others. Even when I feel the fear and self-doubt creeping in, I lean into love. I learn to love myself more and more every day, including all my flaws. This is not about ego; it is showing kindness to yourself and allowing yourself to see the beauty in others.

Trust - learning to trust myself, my decisions and others. It is also trusting the process, which is a big part of the law of attraction. The universe has your back.

What makes you come alive?

Everyone has magic inside of them. I also practice gratitude every day. To focus on what I have already in my life reminds me of how lucky I am. Gratitude centres me.

What self-love rituals do you prioritise and why?

Mediation and gratitude writing. Meditation allows me to connect back to myself, and gratitude writing allows me to be thankful for my life, health, business, and the beautiful people I have in my life.

What is your favourite strategy to unhook from procrastination?

DREAMS + ACTION = REALITY

DREAM: visualise your ideal day. Then, continue to focus on that vision throughout the day—for example, a day filled with love, gratitude and showing up in my full potential.

ACTION: what action do I need to take to make this happen. With every goal/dream I have, I write down 3 actions plans I need to take to make it all become a reality.

REALITY: taking note of the dreams and action is about embodying the feeling I will have when it becomes a reality. We underestimate the importance of these feelings and making sure that it is the feeling you want. Not just what others expect.

What would you say to the women who feel they should be able to do-it-all without a tribe/community/coach?

GO YOU. You are powerful, however, do not feel like you have failed if you need a coach or tribe in the future.

Whose voices do you tune into for a guaranteed dose of inspiration?

Gabby Bernstein, Bob Proctor and Echart Tolle and also my higher self - my own intuition. Tapping back into myself via mediational shows me where I need to be.

What role have coaches and/or masterminds played in your success?

They have played important parts. For example, this year alone, I have worked with 3 coaches, all helping me on different aspects of my life and business.

I believe that coaches/mentors can help everyone. They can inspire you, give you an outside look at your life and business, and show you what you don't want to be.

Do you think you would be where you are now without having worked with a coach and why or why not?

NO. Without their guidance, I don't believe I would be as far ahead as I am in my life or business.

Over the years, I have worked with numerous coaches. All of them have played an essential part. For example, the spiritual coach has allowed me to grow, heal and tap into my intuition; the business mentors have given me essential advice for my business.

What are you most grateful for?

My health and my family. After being diagnosed with 2 life-changing illnesses in 2015, I now never take my health for granted. It gives me the ability to wake up every day and live life to the fullest. It gives me another day to be with my loved ones. It allows me to create the business of my dreams.

What qualities do you see when you say, "She is a PHENOMENAL WOMAN!"?

Strong, Ambitious, Trustworthy, Authentic, Vulnerable, and most of all, Passionate.

Christine Innes Links

instagram.com/christine_innes

facebook.com/christineinnescoach

youtube.com/thecorporateescapists

twitter.com/girlbossau

www.christine-innes.com

www.thecorporateescapists.com

tiktok.com/thecorporateescapists

My health and my family.
After being diagnosed with
2 life-changing illnesses in 2015,
I now never take my health for
granted. It gives me the ability
to wake up every day and live life
to the fullest. It gives me another
day to be with my loved ones.
It allows me to create the business
of my dreams.

CHRISTINE INNES

Caroline Labouchere

A MODEL AND AMBASSADOR FOR HER
GENERATION, REGULARLY REPRESENTING
THE OVER FIFTIES IN PRINT AND FILM.

Caroline Labouchere

A model and ambassador for her
generation. Regularly representing
the over fifties in print and film.

Dubai, United Arab Emirates

*"Compassion is key when dealing with people.
Being empathetic is so much more effective
than sympathy."*

**What has driven you to create the success that you have?
(What is your WHY?).**

I have found my voice. Through unexpected success as a model,
I quickly grew a following who wanted my opinion. Now I am more
about helping others than modelling (although that helps pay the
bills). I am only halfway through my life. There are choices to be
made so that I can walk the talk.

**If you were to choose 3 words that describe who you are as
a woman, what would they be?**

Strong, passionate, happy.

**What role has vision boards and/or clearly defined goals played
in your life and business?**

Affirmations are key to my approach each day. Words next to my
toothbrush help me remember what I want, who I am and where I
am going. I regularly update a vision board. It has served me well,
and as each opportunity arises, I remove the achieved goal and
insert new ones.

**How do you quieten the shame gremlins that say 'who do you
think you are' or 'you're not enough'?**

Imposter syndrome raises its head often. I 'fake it till I make it'
despite feeling uncomfortable at the time. Very quickly, I realise that
I am, I can, I must, I shall... despite internal and external voices that
proclaim the opposite. I don't listen to the shame gremlins anymore;
they are normally wrong and not part of my future success.
Instead, I turn to my husband, who is a reliable source of positive
endorsement and support.

What does living a rich and prosperous life look like to you?

Having the people I love around me. Being loved. Being free and having the luxury of choice with a little bit of security.

Through your feminine lens, what does it mean to be a leader?

Being strong but vulnerable at the same time. Knowing I am not always right, learning from those that know more than me. Standing up for what I believe in. Leading shoulder to shoulder as a team with others.

What role has vulnerability played in your success story?

Huge, if you speak up and share, it helps everyone. Showing up when you don't feel up to it nearly always ends up positively. There is generally a reason, a purpose to everything. I don't think I have a strong ego.

Whether being interviewed or interviewing others, what role have these connected conversations played in your business?

I find knowledge in others and wisdom in sharing it with those who question my parroted truth.

What is the most difficult decision you have had to make to pursue your dreams?

It's not really a decision, or perhaps it is more than one decision... I have had to steel myself to say yes when there is an overwhelming sense that I am stepping into the unknown. But now, saying yes is not a choice nor a decision; it is just what I must do.

What are your core guiding values, and why?

Generosity and kindness. It brings happiness and shines out of your eyes. Compassion is key when dealing with people. Being empathetic is so much more effective than sympathy. I try to get down in the hole with those that I must help.

What makes you come alive?

People. Commercial vice transactional relationships give me energy and optimism.

What self-love rituals do you prioritise and why?

I exercise consistently, with discipline and even when the mood really doesn't support my practice. I feel better if I do and much less energetic when I don't. I don't do self-love as such. I don't do yoga or meditate. I plan to one day. I love to listen to audiobooks with my husband and then discuss them. I love spending time with him.

What is your favourite strategy to unhook from procrastination?

Rituals. And optimism, which for me is consistent, considered, decisive, positive action. Getting stuff done is so much more satisfying for everyone involved. And at the end of the day, there is a sense of achievement and time well spent. I share success and failure with my husband. He clears my head and makes me look at things differently.

What would you say to the women who feel they should be able to do-it-all without a tribe/community/coach?

I say well done if you can do some of it. But no one can do it all; no one is perfect. I like the proverb; if you want to go fast, go alone; if you want to go far, go together. We all have potential forever, whatever our 'forever is. There is no timeline: we should stop only when we are physically unable to go on.

Whose voices do you tune into for a guaranteed dose of inspiration?

My husband. He's kind but strong, full of ideas and experience, and a free hug is included.

What role have coaches and/or masterminds played in your success?

I've experienced coaches, and my husband is (apparently) an excellent and much-reputed coach. But it's all about fit and a little bit of chemistry. For me, I have to understand the coach even more than he needs to understand me. Then the magic happens.

Do you think you would be where you are now without having worked with a coach and why or why not?

Actually, I think that a formal partnership with a coach is not for me. My partnership with my husband sometimes becomes, if only briefly, a coaching relationship. I am also a coach and quickly respond when faced with great questions.

But I find it hard to remain in the role once I realise that I am the coachee! Yes, I probably would be here, but my coaching qualification has helped me ask myself and others questions to which I need answers.

What are you most grateful for?

My husband and children, of course. The people who come into my life, especially now. I love that they are all doing well, that they are happy, balanced, independent and respected.

What are your guilty pleasures?

Diet Pepsi and Cadburys chocolate.

What qualities do you see when you say, "She is a PHENOMENAL WOMAN!"?

I see bravery and grit. A bit of pluck and thick skin are prerequisites of phenomenality! (That's a new word!). I think that Carmen Dell'Orefice is iconic and phenomenal. I intend to get better as I age and hope to model more like her.

Caroline Labouchere Links

📷 *instagram.com/carolinelabouchere*

f *facebook.com/carolinelabouchereisgrey*

🌐 *www.carolinelabouchere.com*

Edwina Murphy-Droomer

THE WISDOM-CURATOR, INTERVIEWER, AUTHOR, VISION BUILDING MENTOR & TRANSFORMATIONAL COACH.

Edwina Murphy-Droomer

The Wisdom-Curator, Interviewer, Author, Vision Building Mentor & Transformational Coach.

Victoria, Australia

"... when I hear how my work has served, inspired and empowered others, that makes my willingness to be vulnerable a superpower, not a weakness."

What has driven you to create the success that you have? (What is your WHY?)

Originally my 'why' was wanting to relieve my husband of being solely responsible for our financial welfare. Having spent many years as a single mother to my four children and only ever having 'just' enough money, my new husband generously poured his finances into our family, with never a complaint. Still, it didn't sit well with me. It was the catalyst that pushed me out of my comfort zone and more determinedly into my entrepreneurial career.

Having achieved that goal, my 'why' has now evolved to create generational wealth to provide security for my children and my grandchildren in years to come. The notion that the coming generations can look back on the legacy I leave and be inspired and proud gives me extra motivation to be even bolder in my work.

If you were to choose 3 words that describe who you are as a woman, what would they be?

Loving, Compassionate, Courageous.

What role has vision boards and/or clearly defined goals played in your life and business?

Pivotal! Having clearly defined goals and a beautiful vision of the future I want to bring to life has been instrumental in supporting me to achieve what I have. In the introduction for this book, I share an example of the role vision boards have played in my business, so I won't repeat it here.

I think of it this way... When planning a wedding, you create a vision for exactly how you want your day to unfold. Every detail from what you will wear, to who you surround yourself with, to the car you will be in, the food you will eat, where you will be, and even the holiday (honeymoon) you will take, every minute detail that is important to you is envisioned.

AND THEN, with a heart full of excited anticipation, you set about bringing that vision to life. As we all know, not every step of that journey is fun nor easy; but you are willing to do whatever it takes to make it a reality.

My feeling is, why not apply that same level of excited anticipation and dedication to your whole life?

How do you quieten the shame gremlins that say 'who do you think you are' or 'you're not enough'?

By picking up the phone and talking to those in my circle of trust.

By reminding myself that my thoughts aren't real, they are just my insecurities surfacing.

By walking away from my work. Taking a break works wonders.

By looking for evidence that it's not true, reflecting on what I have done, the lives I have touched, and the resources I have created.

What does living a rich and prosperous life look like to you?

Being grateful for what I have and relishing in the knowledge that there is always the next level to reach for.

I take no shame in wanting to feel like a Queen. Being in five-star hotels, shopping for luxurious clothes (I have somewhat of an obsession with fine woollen garments and organic fabrics), knowing that I can support sustainable, ethical clothing companies rather than relying on cheap fast fashion is important.

Having access to fresh, organic, locally grown produce.

Time with my husband and my children. Ideally, in front of an open fire with a board game or two, standing side by side in the kitchen preparing a meal, skiing in magical locations, or lounging on a tropical island.

Being a country chick at heart, green rolling hills as far as the eye can see, an orchard filled with fruit trees, a veggie garden bursting with fresh produce, a few chickens, a dog or two, and a garden filled with flowers is my idea of heaven. Oh … and the piece de resistance, fairy lights …lol

All of this without the stress of worrying about paying my bills looks like a rich and prosperous life to me.

Through your feminine lens, what does it mean to be a leader?

Having a strong back and a soft front. (Words inspired by Brene Brown)

Taking 100% responsibility for myself, my choices, and my results.

A willingness to be bold, to speak up and use my voice for the greater good.

A willingness to show up and be seen when I can't control the outcome.

A willingness to have hard conversations with compassion and empathy.

Consciously creating a fault, blame, guilt, shame-free environment.

To make decisions through a filter of love, not fear.

What role has vulnerability played in your success story?

Having experienced heartbreaking grief and having negotiated enormously difficult chapters in my life, I know with certainty that when I have been willing to share the lessons I learned coming out the other side, that my stories have provided comfort and inspiration to others going through similar situations.

There is also enormous vulnerability in putting myself and my work out into the world with little control over how it will be seen or received; opening myself up to the possibility of failure, criticism, and unkind responses is no easy thing.

However, when I hear how my work has served, inspired and empowered others, that makes my willingness to be vulnerable a superpower, not a weakness.

Whether being interviewed or interviewing others, what role have these connected conversations played in your business?

They are the grand centrepiece of all that I create.

They have allowed me to connect with incredible humans in many different countries, to share inspiring conversations and life-changing insights, all whilst building my authority with those who I can serve.

I then have the honour of sharing those conversations with the intention of planting seeds of possibility into the hearts and minds of women across the globe.

I call myself *The Wisdom-Curator,* as that is how I see the work that I now do. Holding the space for women to share their stories and expertise with others so that we all may grow; after all, together, we are so much stronger than we are as individuals.

What is the most difficult decision you have had to make to pursue your dreams?

Investing in my first coach when I didn't have the money. It was a bold, SCARY move, but my instincts told me it was the next best step to get where I wanted to go. That $10,000 investment turned into $135,000 in 12 months, so my gut was right.

What are your core guiding values, and why?

Authenticity, Compassion, Connection, Courage, Freedom, Grace, Health, Humility, Inclusion, Integrity, Love, Nature, Respect, Responsibility, Trust, Vision, Vulnerability, and Wisdom.

What makes you come alive?

Fresh Flowers, Fabulous Food, Fine Fashion, Fairy lights, Farm life, Family and Friends.

I call them my 'F' words!!! LOL

What self-love rituals do you prioritise and why?

Sleep! Becoming a single mother with four children aged between 5 months and 8 years, I know well the benefits of a good night's sleep for both my physical and mental health.

Wearing clothes that make me feel beautiful as it completely transforms how I show up in the world.

Walking barefoot on the grass as it grounds and connects me with mother earth.

A simple but loving moisturizing ritual with natural luxurious products.

Eating organic, locally grown, ethically farmed produce and drinking fresh filtered water because, to me, doing anything else is insanity.

Reading Tosha Silvers Abundance Prayer, which I have on my Vision Board beside my bed because it supports me to be the woman I want to be.

What is your favourite strategy to unhook from procrastination?

Tuning in to the voice of someone who inspires me.

Planning my day early with defined goals.

When I feel stuck, having a shower and restarting my day does wonders.

Focusing on the end result rather than the task in front of me ... i.e. how I will feel when it's done!

What would you say to the women who feel they should be able to do-it-all without a tribe/community/coach? Forget it!

Find your tribe, surround yourself with those who are on a similar path and want to see you succeed.

Find someone who has succeeded in what you want to do and seek to learn from them either via one-on-one or group coaching. (Listening to pre-recorded courses can't possibly get you the same results as human to human conversation.)

Whose voices do you tune into for a guaranteed dose of inspiration?

Brene Brown, Oprah Winfrey, Maya Angelou, Jaimsyne Blakely, & Meredith Allen.

What role have coaches and/or masterminds played in your success?

They have, without question, been the foundation that has supported me to achieve all that I have.

Do you think you would be where you are now without having worked with a coach and why or why not?

There is no doubt in my mind that I would not have achieved all that I have without having worked with a coach. Most of us are filled to overflowing with information, knowledge, and hard-earned wisdom but sadly do little to nothing with it. A coach's job is to pull you forward out of your comfort zone and into implementation and action.

What are you most grateful for?

My children, my husband, and Mother Nature.

What are your guilty pleasures?

Pana Chocolate, Locally baked organic Sourdough Bread, shopping for clothes I don't need but want, having all my children home so I can be like a mother hen and fuss over them, day spa experiences, period dramas (I binge-watched Bridgerton from start to finish in a day), teenage fantasy fiction (my girlfriends had a field day when they found out I loved the Twilight books...lol)

What qualities do you see when you say, "She is a PHENOMENAL WOMAN!"?

I see a woman who is unapologetically all she wants to be.

I see a woman who strives to ensure those around her feel seen, heard and valued.

I see a woman whose beauty comes from an inner strength that is magnetic.

I see a woman who is loving, compassionate and generous.

I see a woman who knows her worth and is dedicated to making the world a better place through the words she speaks and the actions she takes.

Edwina Murphy-Droomer Links

instagram.com/edwinamd

youtube.com/edwinamurphy-droomer

www.edwinamd.com

facebook.com/edwinamurphydroomer

Thorpe-Bowker Identifier Services, official
ISBN Agency of Australia and its territories.

ISBN 978-0-646-84189-2

Design by We Are Purpose

Every business has a story to tell.
We are a design agency passionate about
bringing authentic brand stories to life.

www.wearepurpose.com.au

Authors photographer Adrienne Dillon

www.littleblackrabbit.net

Published by IngramSparks

First printing, July 2021

www.phenomenalfeminineentrepreneurs.com

Printed in the USA
CPSIA information can be obtained
at www.ICGtesting.com
LVHW071533151023
761145LV00006B/140